To Eddie, from his Dad
on our first visit to
Williamsburg - Aug 7, 1959.

REBEL'S ROOST

EARL SCHENCK MIERS

REBEL'S ROOST

The Story of Old Williamsburg

Illustrated by
FRITZ KREDEL

Colonial Williamsburg
1956

For David, Bill and Merry Miers

—*really, for all American boys and girls who
share with them this rich heritage*

REBEL'S ROOST

How It All Started

THE VIRGINIA PENINSULA is a strip of land between the York River and the James River that, rather like a dog's nose, rests its tip against the briny scent of Chesapeake Bay. Beyond, between Cape Charles and Cape Henry, flow the restless tides of the Atlantic Ocean. On a May day in 1607, three little ships passed these capes and carried the first permanent English settlers in America to the sandy beaches of Jamestown; and off these capes, on an October day one hundred and seventy-four years later, the French fleet stood guard while Washington turned the world upside down at Yorktown for Lord Cornwallis and the British redcoats.

Roughly midway in the lazy arc that a duck might fly from Jamestown to Yorktown is Williamsburg, which became the capital of the colony of Virginia in 1699 after fire had destroyed the State House of the original settlement on the James River.

But Jamestown never had been an attractive town. The brackish waters of the swamps surrounding the place bred disease. Its houses were cluttered together like old people seeking shelter in a storm. Williamsburg, at the time it became the capital, was already more than a half century old—a small, sleepy village containing the College of William and Mary, several houses, an ordinary (or tavern), two mills, a smithy, a few stores, a brick church, a graveyard.

Now the old village awakened with a start. Within a few short years Williamsburg grew into a bustling community, especially during the Public Times when the legislature and General Court were in session. Then, as though the old town drew a deep breath and puffed out its cheeks, the population almost doubled overnight. In the shops and taverns, along the dusty streets, across the green grass of Market Square, the crowds gathered—laughing and arguing, drinking and gambling, shouting at the horse races and at the antics of the boys trying to catch the greased pig on Fair Day, passing the laws of the colony and transacting its commercial business. Sometimes, during these exciting days and nights, the inhabitants even caught a few winks of sleep.

Such was the Williamsburg that George Washington came to call his "metropolis." Among his many friends in Williamsburg were Thomas Jefferson, Patrick Henry. Others too would come here, live here—not only rubbing elbows together, but also ideas. Often those ideas were sharp and brittle, seeming to clash like rapiers, and throw off sparks, and presently a fire was kindled by the heat of these sparks. For a time the fire smoldered, but when at last the flame leaped high it became a light seen ultimately around the world. Some called that light revolution, some treason, some liberty. From the ashes of the fire rose a bird—not the phoenix of legend, but the American eagle, symbol of the new nation.

Father decided that we would visit Williamsburg, today restored so that it looks almost as it did during those stirring times. A kind of calamity was behind the whole idea, proof again there is truth in the old saying that it's a very ill wind which doesn't blow good to somebody.

Father looked at my report card, and then he looked at me, pained and reproachful, and I knew what he was thinking—the chip off the old block had disclosed a few bad cracks.

"Why," he asked, "are you failing in American history?"

"It's dry," I said.

"So is a baseball diamond in the middle of the summer," Father said. "You seem to do all right with that."

Then Jane—my sister, I mean—old Pony Tail with the big blue eyes like a cow, breezed into the room.

"Did you see the rotten mark he got in American history?" she asked Father.

Father said, a bit grimly, "I saw it. Moreover, we're going to do something about it."

I've lived through more than one domestic crisis. They take patience. Anyhow, in another week it'd be spring vacation, when things like marks don't mean so much. Or so I thought, until Father said one night: "We'll leave on the afternoon school gets out."

"We're leaving for where?" I asked, thinking of the plans I already had made.

"To get your feet wet in American history," Father said. "So that it won't seem so dry. And you can discover life is more than a ball of string with a horsehide around it."

"And a gutta percha center," Jane added, "like the minds of some people, letting everything bounce on and off."

So that's how it all started. And we came to Williamsburg. And maybe Jane met a ghost. And the three of us really had the time of our lives.

Of course I started off in a grouch—you know how you do, in such cases. When we were driving down the Virginia Peninsula somewhere below Richmond, Father asked:"What does 1749 mean to you?"

"It means you get a penny's change back from seventeen dollars and fifty cents," I grumbled.

"Well, it meant something else to George Washington," Father said. And that's how *he* started. There's nothing wrong with the old block, even if there are cracks in the chip off same.

CHAPTER TWO

Wilderness Trek

T HE LONG JOURNEY from Mount Vernon to Williamsburg required four days of hard riding even when the weather was ideal. George spurred his horse along the narrow road, watching for mud holes, the squealing pigs that sometimes darted from the underbrush, the trees struck down by a thunderstorm two nights before. When at dusk he stopped at a tavern the innkeeper met a young man who at seventeen was shy in manner, yet tall and handsome despite a rather sharp nose.

At daybreak George was back in the saddle, piped along his way by sassy bluejays, chattering squirrels, lilting orioles. Here clearly was a chap who liked to finish without frills or delay whatever he started. Still, riding into the rolling country near Fredericksburg, where the Rappahannock River curved lazily among green hills, George's pace slackened, his thoughts wandered, his heart beat faster.

Most of George's boyhood years had been spent on nearby Ferry Farm. He knew this old river in the way only a boy does after rowing against its tides, sailing its wind-swept bends, swimming its deep, eddying pools. He knew these green hills with a hunter's affection—the fox and wolf tracks, the heavy print of the bear, the old beaver dam, the fleeting glimpse of

the deer. Even after his father had died when George was
eleven he remained at Ferry Farm some time before his half
brother Lawrence asked him to come to live at Mount Vernon.

Lawrence Washington had married a daughter of Lord
Fairfax, so that this crusty old nobleman, visiting Mount
Vernon, cast his first glance at George because he couldn't
avoid it. Down on the Northern Neck, Lord Fairfax was
known for his scowl, his tart tongue, his unsociable dispo-
sition. He was a gruff old bird—hard to the core, some
grumbled—and without an equal on a fox hunt until George
appeared. George's strength and vigor, his ease on a horse,
his quiet shyness all impressed Lord Fairfax. That young
Washington had little formal schooling was obvious to any-

one who ever heard George read aloud, for he seemed to chop off his words with a verbal axe. At spelling the English alphabet became his mortal enemy. But George knew his place in mixed company, and in his own handwriting had taught himself such rules for "decent behavior" as:

> *Sleep not when others Speak, Sit not when others stand, Speak not when you Should hold your Peace, walk not on when others Stop.*

Lord Fairfax liked George, gave him his first job as a surveyor, paid him good wages and helped him to invest his money in property. The old nobleman's interest in seeing George get ahead was behind this journey to Williamsburg. So a confident, determined young man, nourishing bright prospects for the future, clomped down Duke of Gloucester Street, scattering the chickens, ducks and geese, and seeing so much that in later years would be like home to him— Bruton Church where he would often worship, the Palace where he would dine and dance, the Capitol where he would sit as a member of the House of Burgesses.

But George's interest that day in 1749 centered in the College of William and Mary where he must go to win a surveyor's license. The answers he gave must have been satisfactory. He rode home to Mount Vernon with the license in his pocket.

George had rubbed elbows with the sad side of life when he returned to Williamsburg four years later. A voyage to Barbados in the hope that Lawrence might mend in health in the milder climate of the West Indies was behind him now. The scars of the smallpox George had suffered on that journey could be seen on close scrutiny. But in George's eyes were the deeper marks—his grief at the death of Lawrence, the responsibility he carried as the new owner of Mount Vernon. George was twenty-one, already a man, already a leader in the making whose service as an officer in the local militia had revealed the promising military cut of the fellow. Williamsburg in late October of 1753 was in a warlike mood.

Again the old town was bursting at the seams, the streets filled with carriages, the taverns crowded with members of the House of Burgesses called to a special session of the legislature, the air bristling with rumors. Yet Governor Dinwiddie was having his hand forced by the French. No loyal Britisher could stand by, letting those interlopers build forts and occupy the Ohio country that clearly belonged by the King's grant to Virginia.

George and the Governor met at the Palace. Dinwiddie was usually good-humored and benevolent, but today the Governor's blue-gray eyes were sober and resolute. The French must be warned that they were encroaching on British soil. If they had sense and decency, they'd get out. If they didn't, they asked for war.

The journey to the Ohio country to caution the French called for a leader with courage, a stout will, a devoted sense of duty to King and country. How many miles George and his small party must travel to find the French the Governor could not say. He didn't know. The trip might cover a thousand miles. It might take fifteen hundred—almost every mile of it through a country best known for wild Indians, bears and rattlesnakes.

From the window of the Palace the leaves on the trees,

the look of the grass told that the last days of autumn were
fading. November would bring bleak skies, rain, swollen
rivers, cold days and raw nights. December could mean snow,
ice in the rivers, roads frozen and impassable. Yes, George
said, he would lead the expedition and present the Governor's
message to the French. But his mission entailed much more.
He must bring back military information about the country,
in case war came. He must be a diplomat among the Indians,
sounding out their loyalty between the English and French.

The party struck across the mountains carrying guns and
ammunition, tents and food, corn for the horses, medicine,
tobacco, wampum and presents for the Indians, even an
"Indian dress" that Washington might need on ceremonial
occasions. Among the group following the young leader was
Christopher Gist, guide and interpreter, a grizzled old frontiersman who one rainy night had chased a bear from under
a ledge so that he might have a dry place to sleep. As hostlers
and orderlies to the expedition were seasoned men of the
wilderness like Barnaby Currin and John MacQuire, traders
with the Indians. Old Jacob van Braam, who had fought in
the Dutch Army, served George as interpreter.

Presently the party reached rivers whose very names held
terror for a poor speller like George—the Youghiogheny,
the Monongahela. Part of the English grievance against the
French concerned ousting Virginian John Frazier from his
trading post in the Ohio country. Toward mid-November
George reached Turtle Creek where Frazier had set up a new
store.

Frazier was a big, restless fellow, who seemed to feel over-
crowded if he saw his own shadow too often. Yet frontiers-

men liked him, and brought him rifles to repair. He was filled with wilderness news. Three nations of French Indians were spoiling to spill English blood. Governor Dinwiddie depended in part on the friendly Indians of the Six Nations for the defense of Virginia's frontier, but the signs weren't good. True, the Indians of the Six Nations heartily disliked the French and called the English brothers. Still, in a war, could Virginia rely on their allegiance? Frazier didn't know.

George pressed on, intending to find out as much as he could. His eyes judged every wooded hillock he saw along the river banks. Possible sites for forts were weighed in these interludes. And each day found George writing in his journal all he saw and heard so that when he returned to Williamsburg, he could give a full report.

How far away George must have felt from the tidal lowlands of Mount Vernon and the Northern Neck! Already he had crossed mountains three thousand feet above the level of the sea. Forests towered around him—majestic and mysterious, silent and dangerous, a lair of wild animals and wilder Indians. He saw great new rivers. All this was Virginia, this wilderness rolling on and on and having an end no one knew quite where!

In his tent did he dream of the other Virginia that stretched from Mount Vernon to Williamsburg? Some wet, cold nights —for weeks, there seemed to be nothing else—old images must have haunted him. On a plantation a boy grew up, managing his personal servant and gaining confidence in having authority, in using it. Along the road he saw the steeple of the parish church, and a planter's son knew that one day he would take his place on the vestry.

But here in the wilderness, where the John Fraziers lived, was another country. Strong. Rich in promise. Yet untouched by custom, by tradition, by authority or government. Whither would it go—to the English or French? Or was it forever a trapper's outpost, a trader's lonely empire? Whatever were the musings of darkness, daylight routed George from his tent. Usually the trees dripped with the night's rain. The wind cut like a knife and muscles stiffened. Along the trail the horses trudged with lowered heads, buffeting the icy gusts.

In late November George reached Logstown, twenty-five days after leaving Williamsburg. Here he met Monakatoocha, an Oneida and Mingo chief who was also headsman of the Logstown Shawnees. Later Half-King, the Seneca chief, joined them. Unexpected visitors to Logstown were "four or ten" Frenchmen, deserters, who arrived the next day. George learned of four French forts between New Orleans and a place he thought was "Isles Noires" or Black Islands, but no such place existed and the word really was Illinois, then unknown to the English.

The meeting with the Indians continued almost a week. The delay irked George—"waiting here," he wrote in his journal, "was very contrary to my Inclinations"—yet the Indians liked speeches, and made sharp inquiry about Indians held in a Carolina jail, but in the end Half-King proclaimed: "I rely upon you as a Brother ought to do, as you say we are Brothers and one People." Nor did Half-King hold any affection for the French, whom he saw as thieves of the Ohio lands.

George at last pushed on, accompanied by Chiefs Half-King, Jeskakake and White Thunder. Through four days of wretched weather the party sloshed over the road to the Indian town of Venango. Here John Frazier once had owned his house, and they saw it now flying the French colors. Captain Joncaire, who announced he was commander of the Ohio, greeted young Washington pleasantly and invited him to dine. Afterward George wrote diligently in his journal:

"The wine, as they dosed themselves pretty plentifully with it, soon banished the Restraint which at first appeared in their Conversation; and gave a licence to the Tongues to reveal their Sentiments more freely. They told me, That it was their absolute design to take Possession of the Ohio, and by G— they would do it." They would do it, Joncaire said, even if the English could raise two men for their one. Anyhow, the English were slow. While they dawdled, the country would be won.

George listened calmly. Joncaire scoffed openly at Virginia's claim to this territory. LaSalle, a Frenchman, had discovered the Ohio River. George noted each boastful reference to forts reaching up into Canada. At twenty-one he was receiving his first test as a leader, a diplomat. His quiet good sense and resolution, his spunk in the face of threat and danger would remain his best characteristics when, thirty-four years later, he took the oath of office as the first President of a new nation.

Now he was learning—most of all, that diplomacy in the wilderness was a game of cat and mouse. Next day the French tried to woo the three Indian chiefs to their side and with rather a dry humor George wrote in his journal, they "applied Liquor so fast, that they were soon rendered incapable of the Business they came about." George still had to journey on to find St. Pierre, the commander to whom he must deliver Governor Dinwiddie's letter. Snow had begun to fall.

Forty-eight hours later Joncaire and his comrades still were dispensing presents and whisky, and old Christopher Gist watched over the Indians like a hawk. On December 11 the Virginia party finally pushed on, reaching St. Pierre the following day. Again there was a delay. Again the snow fell, the icy winds howled.

George didn't waste time. He studied the fort here on French Creek. Four houses composed its sides. Piles driven into the ground with pointed ends above provided the bastions. George examined the portholes cut for the six-pound cannon, the loopholes through which small arms could fire. Guardhouse, chapel, doctor's lodging, the commander's private store—he noted each along with the platforms where fighting men could stand, the barracks where they lived, the stables, the smithy. He guessed there must be a hundred men at the fort, exclusive of officers. He counted canoes—fifty of birch bark, one hundred and seventy of pine. Others were on frames, blocked-out, ready to be finished in spring.

St. Pierre's answer was what George had expected, advising Governor Dinwiddie: "As to the Summons you send me to retire, I do not think myself obliged to obey it." Inquiry about settlers captured by the French Indians was answered vaguely. Some white scalps had been seen among the Indians —maybe two, three. Two Pennsylvania traders had been taken to Canada but were now released. They had forgotten the name of a boy who had been captured, or the place from which he had been taken.

Meanwhile every trick was being used to win the loyalty of Half-King, White Thunder and Jeskakake. "I can't say that ever in my Life I suffered so much Anxiety as I did in this affair," George confessed in his journal. The snow grew heavier, the horses weakened—clearly the trek home must be made on foot.

Grizzled old Christopher Gist looked at Washington and shook his head, doubting the young leader could make it. But George was expected in Williamsburg. He would get back to Williamsburg.

White Thunder fell ill—with all the whisky around the

fort, it was small wonder—and Half-King declared he must remain to attend him. George knew the risk. With rum, presents, fine speeches the French would try to wheedle the old Indian's favor.

"Don't let the flattery turn you against us," George said, well schooled now in the trickery of the wilderness diplomat.

The weather turned colder. The snow deepened. Ground, creeks, rivers froze. Despite Gist's skeptical glance, George donned "an Indian walking dress" and struck out through the snow. They walked eighteen miles that first day. Gist looked at George striding along, chin out-thrust, gun in hand, pack on back, and changed his mind. The young fellow possessed stamina.

Next day they reached an Indian town on Beaver Creek. Something was wrong—the very air they breathed seemed thick with expectancy. Not fifteen feet away a gun flashed,

and the ball ripped by George and Gist, luckily hitting neither. They leaped for a tree, caught the French Indian who had tried to ambush them, and made him captive.

Yet what could they do with him? At nine o'clock they freed the red varmint. At least they were warned. Other French Indians must be near—to elude them, George and his party walked all night, then, for safety's sake, pressed through the next day until darkenss.

Troubles multiplied. Daylight revealed the Allegheny caked with ice and a day had to be lost building a raft "with but one poor Hatchet"—there was no other way across. The raft floated tipsily, then half way across jammed in the ice. What kept the craft from sinking, neither George nor Gist knew. George put out his setting pole to stop the raft and let the ice pass by.

The current of the Allegheny struck the pole. George felt its violent quiver, then the pole gave and jerked George with it. He saw the sky overhead before he struck the water. He was in over his head, chilled to the bone. He saw a raft log and grabbed for it. Clearly they couldn't reach either shore, but an island gave them a refuge.

With daylight the Virginians escaped from the island, crossing on the ice. All of Gist's fingers and some of his toes were frozen. Another morning brought them to John Frazier's store, and George found a grisly tale to relate:

"We met here about 20 Warriors who were going to the Southward to War, but coming to a place upon the Head of the great Kunnaway [that is, the Great Kanawha River], where they found seven People killed and scalped (all but one Woman with very light Hair) they turned about and ran back for fear the Inhabitants should rise and take them as the Authors of the Murder. They report that the Bodies were lying about the House, and some of them much torn and eaten by Hogs. By the Marks which were left, they say they were French Indians of the Ottaway Nation, &c., who did it."

The Indian Queen Aliquippa of the Delawares had feared for George's safety in visiting the French, and George traveled three miles to the mouth of the Youghiogheny (George spelled it Yaughyaughane) to tell her of his return. He took her a matchcoat and a bottle of rum. The liquor pleased her greatly. Back at Frazier's George secured horse and saddle and on New Year's Day resumed his journey home. On the sixteenth of January he was back in Williamsburg.

Father closed the book from which he had read Washington's account of his journey into the Ohio country. It was late afternoon of our first day in Williamsburg, and Jane said, "This really was Washington's town by adoption!"

"A lot of Washington is here," Father agreed. "The long and bloody French and Indian War was to follow, with Braddock's costly defeat at Fort Duquesne, but Washington still would prove that he could cling to the habit of finishing what he started. He was sent out as a surveyor of the ground where Braddock fared so badly. And one day he stood among the smoldering embers of Fort Duquesne and planted there with pride and defiance the British flag!"

Yes, I thought, he would—just as he had taken that raft across the ice-packed Allegheny and one Christmas night would pay a surprise visit on the Hessians across the ice-

packed Delaware at Trenton! Somehow, you could feel
Washington growing on that mission to warn the French—
you could feel him taking the measure of their fort right
down to the last canoe blocked-out and waiting to be floated,
and taking the measure also of Half-King and Joncaire and
St. Pierre, and old Christopher Gist, who would learn how
well a twenty-one-year-old Virginian from the Northern
Neck could travel frozen mountain trails!

But there was something more, when you dug into the
facts. There wasn't any feeling then but a sense of loyalty to
Britain—here in Williamsburg or in the wilderness of Turtle
Creek where John Frazier repaired rifles for frontiersmen.
No one really thought of himself as an American—that came
later and it made you wonder why and how and what was
behind the change, in a man like Washington most of all.

Here was a kind of mystery and I wanted to know the
answer. And then my sister encountered another mystery,
and the two puzzles went together in a sense.

CHAPTER THREE

The Ghost of Williamsburg

J ANE DISCOVERED that Williamsburg possessed a ghost. Toward dusk one evening, walking alone down Duke of Gloucester Street, she was startled by the growl of a dog. A large, ugly looking brute, lurking in the shadows between two houses, glared at her with dark, smoldering eyes.

Again the dog growled, deeply, sinisterly. Jane felt rooted to the spot.

It was then that the old gentleman appeared. Once more Jane felt startled, for, seemingly, the old fellow had popped from out of nowhere. Walking along with one hand holding the other behind his back, there was a pensive, meditative air about the man as though his thoughts were miles away from Jane and the dog.

Yet in a glance he understood the situation. He spoke softly to the dog, then held out his hand. The growls ceased and, after a tentative wag of his tail, the animal lifted its head to be petted.

"There, see, it's all right," the old gentleman told Jane. "You surprised him and he surprised you, just as you and I surprised each other meeting here, but now we can all be friends."

Father interrupted Jane's story, asking, "How big was this man?"

"About middle size."

"With a head that was rather round? Did he have quite a large nose and sharp indentations running down his cheeks —I mean the sunken appearance old men get when they lose their teeth?"

Jane looked strangely at Father. "Why, that's so!"

"Which way did he go?"

"I—I'm not sure," Jane said. "I was looking at the dog, and beginning to make friends with it, and when I glanced up the old gentleman had vanished."

Father smiled, principally to himself. "Of course it was all only a coincidence," he decided. "Even if the description and mannerisms fit, and even if there are those who believe in this Williamsburg ghost, I don't hold with this supernatural business. Anyhow, that ghost isn't supposed to leave his own house—he has no right to spoil a legend by being off bounds that way." And Father laughed, adding, "Well, if one *has* to meet a ghost, then one might as well take up with one who in life was a wise and noble man."

Exasperated at the whole silly mystery, I asked: "Whose ghost, for Pete's sake?"

Father said, pronouncing the name as though it rhymed with Smith, "The ghost of George Wythe! If there is such a ghost, it's a good one, for alive George Wythe was one of the most remarkable men ever to live in America. To tell the truth, he did have a round head and a large nose and indentations in his cheeks and the surliest kind of dog came running up to him to be petted!"

Father declared that had he lived in Williamsburg in the old days he would rather have had Wythe for a friend than almost anyone else. He was the sort of gentle, mild-mannered man children trusted and flocked around, bringing him their problems—and their mouths blackened from chewing Spanish licorice. Always Wythe had some young person under his wing, helping him get a start in life. He became the friend, the tutor, the confidant of any number of youths who would become famous in history—Henry Clay, Chief Justice John Marshall, Edmund Randolph.

And of course a very unusual young man named Thomas Jefferson.

"Those old patriots were all thick as thieves," Jane said, somewhat critically.

But Father replied that Jane was wrong if she thought they all had been snipped from the same piece of cloth. They were rugged individuals, those fellows. There just weren't two like Jefferson—or George Wythe, for that matter.

Winter or summer, Wythe's day always began the same way. Before the sun was up, out of the door leaped Wythe. At the well he drew the buckets of water for his morning shower bath, and, when the reservoir was full, yanked the cord. Light sleepers in Williamsburg must have heard him some mornings, gasping for breath and all but shouting against the shock of that icy well water.

Every nerve tingling now, Wythe dashed back to the house swearing that he had never felt better and calling for his breakfast. Yet he was not a typical Williamsburg man, thinking he was underfed unless he consumed most of a pig before sunrise. Compared to those who believed they had not breakfasted at all without a portion of ham and bacon and spareribs and hot bread and eggs and cereal and molasses, he was rather a finicky eater. Eggs, toast and coffee satisfied him.

All days were busy for George Wythe. He was a member of the House of Burgesses, one of the colony's most gifted attorneys and justices. When, feeling fit as a fiddle, he emerged for the day's work from his fine brick house on the west side of the Palace Green, he walked exactly like the old gentleman Jane had seen—hands behind his back, holding one in the other. His sharp blue eyes noticed everything—a new pair of square-toed shoes, the fashion of the day (and only the devil could tell the right foot from the left); a public sale of slaves on the steps of Raleigh Tavern; a builder who was making a mistake putting square-ended shingles on his roof, for they always warped and curled when they dried too quickly in the Virginia sun. Most of all, he never missed a new and interesting face.

During 1760 Wythe became drawn increasingly to one face which had made its first appearance in Williamsburg that year. Tom Jefferson was seventeen then, a rail of a boy standing well over six feet who had come out of the rolling upland mountains to attend William and Mary. His hair was often described as carrot-hued, and seeing Tom trotting down Duke of Gloucester Street an observer like Wythe easily might decide that thin, gawky young Jefferson resembled nothing so much as a carrot that had sprouted arms and legs.

Yet anyone taking a sharper look at Tom Jefferson could have seen that here was no giddy-headed youngster. Tom's mouth was firm and confident, his gaze steady, his chin square and stubborn. There was a sun-ripened tautness to his skin, the look of a lad who liked hunting and fishing, who could handle a horse like a veteran, and who could chase the wiliest fox to its lair. There was another characteristic in Tom—his quick, restless hazel-gray eyes gave it away—a kind of innate curiosity that came out in odd ways. Growing up, he would be gone one day digging up bones in an old Indian burial ground. Next day he would be found soberly timing himself to see how quickly he could walk a mile.

At the age of fifteen, upon the death of his father, Tom inherited the management of Shadwell, the Jefferson plantation near Charlottesville. The lad was equal to the responsibility. Tobacco ripened in the fields and was harvested. House and barns were put in good repair. And at a nearby school Tom prepared himself for college, and discovered even then that girls could be a confounded problem.

Attending the dances, the horse races, a cock fight (poor sensitive Jefferson watched only one, for that vicious sport disgusted him), he gave Williamsburg a new name. To Tom, writing home with a picture in his mind of the gambling and drinking and roistering that went on during Public Times, the capital should have been called "Devilsburg."

Pangs of conscience seemed to nibble at Tom like a mouse with a wedge of cheese. Some days he would study for fifteen or sixteen hours. He drove a stake in the ground about a mile from the college and for exercise appeared each evening to run to that point and back.

Now there was a sight. Think of crowded Williamsburg during Public Times—the shops busy, the taverns so jammed men took turns sleeping in the same bed, the streets teeming with rumbling coaches from which ladies in feathers and fine

silks looked out in astonishment upon Jefferson, this animated
human carrot, long thin nose in the air, elbows flailing at his
sides, skinny legs bobbing up and down as he took his breather
between lessons!

George Wythe wasn't one to miss a sight like that. There
were many qualities in Jefferson to whet Wythe's curiosity.
He stood at the top of his class at the college. From all reports

Tom possessed a mind that soaked up knowledge like a sponge and gave back all sorts of lively ideas when that mental sponge was squeezed. In two years Jefferson completed his studies at William and Mary. By then Wythe and he were warm friends.

About 1762 Thomas Jefferson began to study law under George Wythe, certainly no enterprise for a slacker. After that cold shower before dawn, Wythe was ready to receive a student by sunrise. Then Wythe prowled through his library, looking over his books, seizing a volume that caught his fancy, opening it. There was the lesson. With George Wythe listening, no student skipped over a name, a historical fact, a quotation, an allusion. Who *was* the person, what *had* happened, who *did* say it, what did the allusion *mean*? A student explained these things, or looked them up. Since neither was going to sit down to breakfast until Wythe was satisfied, diligence became the better part of a full belly!

To Tom it was wonderful. Wythe, who even taught one of his Negro slaves to read Latin and Greek, gave life to every page his breath touched. Algebraic equations, French, literature, law—like a plow, Wythe's mind furrowed deeply all these fields of learning, turning up hidden riches. To Jefferson, studying law, the old tutor gave the advice he told all who studied under him. Don't skim! Read deeply! Ponder what you read!

Tom, then only twenty, was bursting to know everything. As though borne on a magic carpet, he trod the soft grass of the Palace Green to the brick mansion where Wythe lived. By the gate, up the steps, through the door—and into a world that grew larger, larger.

For George Wythe was not just a book walking in velvet

breeches and a ruffled shirt. He loved people. Governor Francis
Fauquier was his friend, Tom's friend. There were evenings
at the Palace when Tom brought his violin and the Governor
played the harpsichord. Another friend was William Small,
Professor of Natural Philosophy at the college. Above the
tree tops was a world that only the birds were supposed to
have glimpsed, but Professor Small could describe it. He had
been up in a balloon.

Yet George Wythe was the deep influence on Jefferson,
the lasting teacher. Ideas passed so naturally between them
that it was not always easy to tell which belonged to the other.
When Tom practiced law in later years, his meticulous prep-
aration of every case was a habit Wythe taught and practiced.
Once the two argued opposite sides of a case.

The year now was 1770, and Jefferson's own ideas about
the law were taking shape, as though his mind were filling
out along with his shoulders and arms and legs. He was growing in four dimensions—up and down and in and out. To
Tom an old law was not necessarily a good law. As Jefferson
grew in sympathy and understanding for people, so did his
notions of law develop. Abuses of passion, as when two angry
men settled their quarrel on the duelling ground, should be
stopped by law. Yet weakness of human nature, as when a
woman with a loose tongue gossiped too much and was
ducked in the public pond, could be punished too harshly,
or in a spirit of vicious ridicule.

In this conviction that law must protect human rights,
Jefferson accepted the case of Sam Howell, a young mulatto
boy who was indentured to a Mr. Netherland. In 1723 a
Virginia law had declared that a child born of a bound mulatto

woman was also to be indentured. But Sam Howell was the *grandson* of such a parent—and he contended, therefore, that he should be free under the law.

On Court Day, Tom suffered the annoyance of a cone-shaped breathing tube held over his nose while the barber powdered his wig. In a judicial gown, he entered the room a figure of sedate and gloomy apprehensions. His glance fell nervously on George Wythe, who was defending Mr. Netherland. Wythe appeared calm, cool, confident—a smile on his clean-shaven face, a twinkle in his blue eyes, and not a ripple in the high forehead that gave him an air of enormous wisdom.

Jefferson arose to address the court. He admitted that under the law of Virginia the sons and daughters of parents in bondage were also bound. Then Tom struck out on his own, speaking of a law above the law of Virginia—the law of nature under which "all men are free."

God was the Author of this law of nature, Jefferson told a frowning judge, flinging a challenge at the court—at the whole colony of Virginia.

"So that the position at first laid down is proven, that the act of 1705 makes servants of the first mulatto, that of 1723, extends it to her children, but that it remains for future legislation, if any shall be found wicked enough, to extend it to the grandchildren."

George Wythe was never called to defend his client. When Jefferson finished, the court said icily, "The case is dismissed."

Tom had said, "All men are born free," and in the Declaration of Independence he would write, "All men are created equal." Wythe, who had taught one slave to read Latin and

Greek and in his will would free all his slaves, remained Tom's
friend, Tom's tutor. In court, as fellow members of the House
of Burgesses and later of the Continental Congress, as patriots
and devoted friends of Washington, the years ahead beckoned
to the teacher and the pupil.

Jane squirmed uneasily. "I thought," she said, "that only
people involved in violence left ghosts behind them."

If that were true, Father answered, then Williamsburg had
a right to claim its ghost. George Wythe died in agony, a
victim of deliberate murder. A grand nephew, George Wythe
Sweeney, deeply entangled in financial difficulties, placed arsenic in strawberries. A servant, who ate the poisoned fruit,
died quickly, but Wythe lingered on for a week—long enough
to disinherit the villainous Sweeney.

"Did they hang him?" Jane cried.

Father shook his head. Only a servant had seen Sweeney
with the arsenic. "Under Virginia law," Father said drily,
"a slave could not testify."

Later that night I shivered, trying to fall asleep but thinking instead of that fellow Sweeney. Then off in the distance
I heard a dog howling, a mournful, drawn-out sound. The
night became silent again, but I waited, suddenly tense, ex-
pectant. Presently I heard a series of barks—the kind a dog
makes when its tail begins to wag at the sight of a friend.

I simply wondered, that was all. If there were a ghost in
Williamsburg, he was still mighty popular.

And maybe this ghost business had absolutely nothing to
do with the fact that next morning we found ourselves wan-
dering through a graveyard.

CHAPTER FOUR

The Governor's Silver

THE GIRL WAS named Anne and the boy called
Peter. In the peaceful yard of old Bruton Church,
we found the ivy-covered graves, the weathered
tombstones. Was Peter the young silversmith's apprentice
with the unruly black hair and brown, good-humored eyes
whom George Washington noticed with amusement on the
day he ordered the garnet ring for Patsy Custis, his step-
daughter? And did Anne own the saucy nose beneath the
sunbonnet that every merchant in Williamsburg viewed with
a slight shudder, for the young imp drove a hard bargain?

We could imagine, Father said, that Peter was this boy
and Anne this girl. Actually, they were more important in
history than Washington or Wythe or Jefferson. They had
grown up, built homes of their own, raised families, died.
And some had taken up arms and fought for freedom, or
there could have been no Revolution. They were like us,
this Anne and Peter, just as Father was like their fathers,
complaining from time to time that nowadays all children
were headstrong, self-centered, spoiled.

Every colonial household with youngsters growing up
heard that grumbled complaint. Chores and lessons were
neglected unless parents kept a sharp watch. All the girls

wanted to dance, and even in a man's own kitchen servants could be found teaching his daughters how to jig. And the boys all talked of hunting and fishing, or wanted to go to the horse races, or whispered over what you could see in the taverns at night—planters with more money than sense playing dice, billiards, cards and drinking themselves groggy on ales, Madeira wine and old Barbados rum. That Burdette's

Ordinary was a lively place—the crowd who passed through the door under the swinging sign of Edinburgh Castle didn't go there to discuss Greek mythology.

So the boys whispered and the girls learned to jig as well as to sew and weave and cook, and somehow for all the tomfoolery at the day's end most of the lessons were learned, the chores discharged. "Underneath they're good children," colonial parents said, more indulgent on second thought. An English visitor to Williamsburg had to write home, with real regret, that there could be no question of it—the children here were shamefully pampered.

But off on a morning's marketing, Anne didn't think so. Her bright blue eyes swept over the signs before the shops, put there to help those who couldn't read—the three sugar loaves that were the traditional symbol of the colonial grocer, the boot that marked the cobbler's shop, the unicorn's horn that proclaimed John Carter dealt in a variety of merchandise, including "Mrs. Rednap's red fit drops" which Anne hoped she would never need. But John Carter sold —"for ready money only," and that was his policy, take it or leave it — things Anne could get nowhere else. Ink powder. Castile soap. The Rhenish wine her father liked.

Entering John Carter's store, Anne saw the golden ball over the shop where Peter worked as an apprentice. Oh, she knew him all right—a sassy boy with thirty-seven freckles on his nose; she had counted them to keep awake during church service. She really knew very little otherwise about Peter—except that he was two years older than she, that he had lived on a farm in the western country toward Fredericksburg, that George Wythe was teaching him algebraic equations, and that he had heard Washington ordering the garnet ring for Patsy Custis.

"You stop by at the shop and I'll show it to you," Peter had offered after church. Ann had seen then the two freckles she hadn't counted before—rather a splotched-up nose, come to think of it.

At the silversmith's shop, the lad with the splotched-up nose decided she would come. Now sixteen, Peter had served four of his seven years as an apprentice and had learned at least what appealed to a young lady's fancy. He had learned also that he would earn a smart tongue-lacing if he let the fire in the forge run low for want of charcoal. Whether or not he missed Anne, he'd have to trot over to the baker for another sack of the stuff. The baker would have it all right— he couldn't heat his ovens without producing charcoal—but the longer delay would be fetching the cakes and ale for the mid-morning break. All Williamsburg, Peter thought grump-ily, lived for its stomach.

Peter returned, puffing. Yet a guarded inquiry reassured him. No one had called.

After a few minutes work in the shop resumed. At the forge the smith called over his shoulder, "Be a good lad, Peter, and fetch me Nell." Obediently Peter went to the rack and took down a two-pound hammer. That was "Nell," for a silversmith was by habit a fellow who always made his energy count and by giving pet names to his tools he could call for them without long descriptions of the precise tools he wanted. So "Nell," the two-pounder with a convex face and nick on the right side, spent her idle time on the rack between lighter "Aunt Jen" and heavier "Uncle Moses."

Yet just for an instant, holding the hammer, Peter lost heart. How could he ever accumulate all the equipment to be a silversmith in his own right? The forge. The ingot molds. The tongs and pliers, the punches, the dozens of hammers named "Tom" and "Mary" and "George the III" for that square-headed Stamp Act—it would take forever.

Peter gave himself a shake. Time, toil, thrift—he would be only nineteen when he completed his apprenticeship, as strong as an ox and free to go as he pleased. Others had started from scratch and made a place for themselves. Why shouldn't he? How else did a colony like Virginia go on growing every year?

The smith reached out for "Nell," balanced the hammer in his hand, and broke into a smile. "Peter, lad, we'll be finished this afternoon," he said in a gay spirit, "and ye'll be taking this set of silver plate to the Palace to deliver to the Governor."

The boy nodded, catching the smith's eagerness, his excitement. For weeks they had labored on the silver plate. In Peter's mind every painstaking step of the work was clear, logical, a part of an adventure. For Peter to watch the hammers falling on a silver ingot was an unfolding miracle. Bit by bit the shape emerged, almost like the blossom of a crocus opening in spring. "Fetch me Nell...fetch me Uncle Moses" —each command had meaning as the flat plate was hollowed and acquired purpose and form. Then the filing, and the rough edges disappeared until the plate became rounded and soft under the touch of the fingers.

"What think ye, Peter?" the smith asked, holding up a finished plate.

" 'Tis fine," the apprentice said. And "fine" was the only word to use, a simple word to describe the beauty of plain and unaffected craftsmanship, as "fine" was the word for the simple wonder of changing color in Williamsburg—the black-green boxwood in spring, the brilliant daylilies in summer, the red of the Virginia creeper in autumn, the dark marl along the walks in winter. Watching Peter, why did the smith smile? And nod? Was it because some poets write verses and others fashion plates for the table of the Governor's Palace?

With a start Peter looked up to see Anne standing in the shop. A bit sheepishly, showing her the garnet ring Washington had ordered, he explained about the silver plate for the Governor.

"Will you come with me?" Peter asked. "I'll be driving over about five o'clock this afternoon."

Anne tried to seem noncommittal. She had never been in the Palace. "We'll see," she said, and felt almost angry because she could tell that Peter already had guessed where impulse would lead her.

Anne hurried home along Francis Street, for her family lived on the corner beyond John Chiswell's house with the high, English-style roof that looked out of place in Williamsburg. There wasn't another like it in town, ot anyone quite like Colonel Chiswell for frightening her with his fierce dark eyes—and frightening her with good reason too, for in another year Colonel Chiswell would be marched off to jail for killing a merchant in a fit of rage.

The girl found Eliza, the colored cook, in the backyard kitchen house. As usual Eliza was full of complaints.

"Miss Anne, you get that Greenhow's tincture fo' my teeth?"

"Yes, I did, and if you'd stop cracking walnuts with them they wouldn't ache so much."

"Lawd, Miss Anne, I don't have time fo' getting a hammer," Eliza grumbled, sitting in a shoo-fly chair and working a pedal with her foot so that, above her head, a fan connected by a rod to the chair swished back and forth. "All there's time fo' round this kitchen is cook, cook, cook!"

Eliza's grumpy face made Anne laugh. The big fireplace transformed the kitchen into a sweltering inferno, but Eliza had her fire at a high, hot flame to sear the beef before she roasted it. The kettle bubbled with Scotch barley broth. Dinner, the big meal of the day, was served at two-thirty, and the fact that Eliza had worked diligently that morning could not be denied. With the beef soon to be roasted and the simmering broth were a baked ham, roasted oysters, cabbage, tarts, hot bread, custard. They wouldn't starve.

Eliza shelled peas, kept pushing the treadle on the shoo-fly chair, and stared at a copy of last week's *Virginia Gazette* spread on the floor. Eliza couldn't read, but she mumbled as though she could. Anyhow, Eliza always liked to look for the picture of a Negro in flight that adorned the advertisements for runaway slaves. She didn't have to be told who they were. She always knew—how far in advance was anybody's guess.

Anne went across the walk to the house. The cleaning up maid was in the parlor polishing the Chinese porcelain tea set—she never missed a day. For two years the maid hadn't smiled, not since her husband Sam, learning the cobbler's trade, had taken to the heels he made for himself. Well, thought Anne, teach a slave a trade and probably you could wave good-bye to him. Or so the planters said.

In the back room off the parlor Anne found her mother at the spinning wheel. The girl had meant to practice on the harpsichord till dinner, but now she decided to get her embroidery and join the older woman. Anne's mother had been wheedled this way before. An attentive daughter usually became a coaxing daughter.

"What favor now?"

"Can I go with Peter to the Palace? He—he's delivering the new silver plate for the Governor!"

"I suppose, if—"

Anne understood. If her father said yes. There was only one master in any Williamsburg house. "I'll ask him after dinner," she promised. And bless John Carter for still having bottles of that Rhenish wine.

It was almost five when the smith loaded the plates in the carriage and Peter seized the reins. Two fine bay mares in the harness picked up their ears.

"Mind that ye behave properly," the smith warned sharply. "Don't gawp if they let ye into the Palace. And don't go snooping into rooms where ye're not invited."

Peter swallowed, a bit uncomfortably. If he did meet Anne, and she went to the Palace with him, gawping and snooping were likely to be her chief interests. Peter flicked the reins and the carriage began to roll along Duke of Gloucester Street. His guess was that Anne would be waiting at the entrance to the Palace Green. He was torn now over whether he wished to see her at all. No apprentice could afford the ill will of his master, even if an attractive lass were at the root of his discomfiture.

Dust rose in clouds from under the turning carriage wheels. Peter choked, brushed a fly from his nose, and looked quizzically down the street for Anne. No sight of her yet—did he feel relief or regret?

On the step before the office of the *Virginia Gazette* a boy in an apron with an ink-stained face fanned himself with an

old newspaper. Four men were bowling beside Market Square
Tavern. A cheering crowd had gathered around the players,
waving their hats and clay pipes at each good bowl—and one
almost losing his wig in a shuffle of excitement. Peter supposed
that they were merchants or planters, settling some sort of
bet.

Anne waited at the corner where Duke of Gloucester
Street joined the Palace Green. She was dressed in silk ruffles
and a lace collar—anyone would think that she expected to
be presented to the Governor. But in sudden good-humor
Peter helped her into the carriage and said honestly, "I'm
glad you're here."

"Well, you can thank Father's Rhenish wine for that," she said, and then laughed. "What a lot of ducks men are, honking and flapping their wings and then when they get their bellies wet as peaceful and contented as cherubs."

At the gate to the Palace a servant stopped them. He was a tall, gruff fellow, and in uniform he looked a proper symbol of the authority of the British crown for which the Palace stood. On the other hand, Peter suspected, Anne saw him as just another duck preparing to honk and flap his wings.

Honk the servant certainly did, in the voice of an Old Testament prophet, suggesting at least eternal brimstone for Peter unless he waited exactly where he was until the man secured permission for him to enter the Palace. In a few minutes he returned, saying the Governor would receive the silver plate. He was obviously disappointed that he couldn't jail Peter on the spot.

A bit breathlessly, carrying the silver and Anne tagging at his heels, the young apprentice entered the main hall of the Palace. Anne gawped at the rich woodwork of carved black walnut. Over the mantel, of oak, the Royal coat of arms met their gaze. Muskets leaned against the wall, another symbol of the authority of the crown. Despite the smith's warning, Peter sneaked a glimpse into the front parlor. He saw the little ivory fishes used as counters set up on a card table for a game of loo. Porcelain figurines of wild birds graced the mantle. There was a portrait hanging on the wall. Anne, snooping, found the family dining room across the hall where, some evenings, George Wythe, young Thomas Jefferson and Professor Small dined with the Governor. The brocade drapes were lovely, Anne thought. She looked too into the warming room, where the food was kept hot after it was brought from the outside kitchen.

Peter had moved down for a glimpse of the state dining room, and his heart as a young silversmith had just bounded at the fine wall sconces for the candles and at the urn on the serving table, when a servant said crossly, "The Governor will see you in his study upstairs. Please *follow* me."

Peter glanced worriedly at Anne, but she seemed undisturbed that they had been caught red-handed. Rather, she was marveling at the staircase—the widest, she had heard, in Virginia—and then, reaching the first landing, she marveled anew at the inlaid replicas carved of boxwood that covered the nail holes on the edge of the treads. Each stood for a different suit in a deck of playing cards—hearts and spades, diamonds and clubs.

"Isn't it wonderful?" she whispered to Peter.

His puckered mouth warned: "Ss*sh*!"

"Will the Governor strike me dead if I open my mouth in his Palace?" Anne asked, irritably and loudly.

"Indeed, he will not," said a pleasant voice in the upper hall. Peter gulped and Anne's face crimsoned.

Francis Fauquier was a handsome man with a kind countenance and gentle eyes. His smile was quick and infectious and invariably drew people to him. And now he said to Anne, "Come with me and I'll show you a pretty sight."

He led her to the parlor. Hand-tooled leather covered the walls, the furnishings were rich and beautiful. But the Governor wanted Anne to see the Palace Green from the window. Catalpa trees bordered that long green vista. Anne caught her breath and the Governor smiled.

Peter saw the bedchamber beyond—the seven razors on the windowsill, a different one for each day as befitted the dignity of the crown's whiskers, the boy supposed. And at last they did reach the Governor's study, and he did examine the silver plates and pronounce them as fine as any he could have secured in England. Peter tried not to show how his mouth tightened. Why shouldn't they be?

Again Governor Fauquier seemed deeply interested in Anne. "Would you like to see the ballroom?"

"Oh, I'd love to!"

"Then let me show it to you."

Descending the staircase once more, Peter knew it was silly of him to feel cross. He should be proud and not half jealous because Governor Fauquier acted so gallantly toward Anne. The Governor after all was a great gentleman. And what did Peter care? But if he didn't care, then he felt cross over feeling cross. "You're a fool," he told himself, peevish also at this admission.

The ballroom was the grandest room Anne ever had seen. Here, Williamsburg gossips insisted, George Washington danced for hours without tiring. Anne could believe it. Closing her eyes, she could see the ladies in their satin and brocade gowns, the candles flickering in the crystal candelabras, the couples swirling around and around to the soft music—it would be like floating on clouds. The gentlemen holding their punch glasses, bowing graciously, smiling— she hated really to open her eyes, but Peter tugged impatiently at her arm.

Then in far too short a time they were outside, where the gruff servant could look them over with the liquid glance of a suspicious hound dog. Anne, sensing Peter's crossness, stared at him intently. All at once she burst out laughing.

"Peter, you're an impossible boy," she declared.

"Why, I should like to know?"

"Because," she said, not the least awed by his scowl, "when I counted on Sunday there were only thirty-seven freckles on your nose. Now there are forty-one!"

As Father said, standing in the yard of Bruton Church and looking down at the old graves, as long as we were going to imagine a day in the life of Peter and Anne we might as well imagine a good one. It had been a good day for Governor Fauquier too—and Father could think of some that had been quite the opposite.

CHAPTER FIVE

The Son of Thunder

W E SAT ON A BENCH under the old tree across the street from Market Square. Morning sunlight speckled the brick walks along Duke of Gloucester Street. A boy on a bicycle whistled shrilly as he rode down the path toward the Guardhouse and Powder Magazine. Jane's curious glance followed the boy, and the sun, falling on her upturned nose, didn't miss a freckle.

The British Great Union flag flapped on the flagpole in front of the Powder Magazine. Fear of Indian attacks, of slave uprisings, of local riots, and of raids from pirates or enemy privateers had led to the building of this strange, eight-sided arsenal in 1715.

"When Washington rode back from the French and Indian War, the old arsenal must have looked just like that," I told Father.

"It was a landmark to anyone visiting Williamsburg," he agreed. "Jane may complain that the old patriots were like peas in a pod, but that isn't so. Most of all, they had minds of their own. By here one day rode a chap on his way to take his seat in the House of Burgesses who woke up Williamsburg with such a start that soon they were calling him the Son of Thunder."

"Who was he?" Jane asked, never able to wait for anything.

"He had ridden down from Louisa County, over in the Piedmont," Father said. "He wore his sandy hair in a greased pigtail and his bony frame was clad in homespun. Riding along Duke of Gloucester Street on an underfed sorrel horse, he looked like a back-country bumpkin."

"Who, Papa? *Who*?" Jane kept pestering, until I wished that the fellow who fired the cannon at the Powder Magazine would clonk her on the head with an iron ball.

But all that thing did was make a racket, and Jane continued sounding like a screech owl with her "Who, Papa? *Who*?"

So Father said, "The rider was Patrick Henry."

Of course Jane tried to start an argument: "He wore a wig, Papa. I've seen a picture of him—one with his eyeglasses pushed up on his forehead—and he has a wig."

"That picture was painted many years later," Father said, "after fiery Patrick had cooled off and been elected Governor of Virginia. I'm talking of a May day in 1765—back in the time when Williamsburg's other great redhead, Tom Jefferson, was studying law."

Patrick Henry was then twenty-nine years old. Some claimed, then and later, that Patrick was one of the laziest men in Virginia, but they should have looked again at this Scotsman's stubborn, out-thrust jaw. The streak of a fighting terrier was in this fellow.

Hard luck had been about all Patrick Henry had known to this point in life—most of it of his own making. Growing up in those western backwoods, he had hated setting and worming tobacco and couldn't escape from such work soon enough. So at the age of fifteen he decided to become a store clerk, and after a time Patrick and his brother William set up a crossroads store. Many folk believed that you couldn't find a better fiddler than Patrick in all of Louisa County. He could tell a story better than most. But at keeping a store—well, in less than a year he and William were broke.

At eighteen Patrick married and returned to farming. He had six slaves to help him, but they couldn't change the fact that his three hundred acres of land were mostly sandy and worn out, or that the nearest river transportation was about ten miles away. After three years even Patrick had to recognize that he was more gifted at fiddling than farming. A fire destroyed his house and furniture but he had been ready to quit, anyhow.

There were youngsters around the Henry household now.

Patrick and his wife decided to open another store, and for two years watched the debts pile up. Only the field mice must have been steady customers, and convinced at last that he would never make a good merchant, he closed up the place.

The situation wasn't so bad as it sounded. Patrick Henry's father-in-law owned a tavern and the family at least had a roof over their heads and something in their stomachs. The point was, what should Patrick try next? Maybe he could become a lawyer—there wasn't much choice left. For six weeks he studied the law books, then appeared for his examination.

Among those who examined Patrick that day was Tom Jefferson's friend and tutor, George Wythe. Looking down at this hayseed lawyer-to-be, Wythe may have bitten his tongue against the temptation to tell this young man that a good cold shower every morning might wake him up to the realities of life. Law required diligent study, not a quick poke of the nose in a few books. Likely Patrick said, "Yes, sir—I intend to keep studying, sir," and he must have said so convincingly for Wythe signed the license that made him Patrick Henry, Attorney-at-Law.

If Patrick was lazy, then it was a funny kind of laziness, for in the next three years he managed almost twelve hundred cases. All over that poor region between Hanover Courthouse and Fredericksburg people liked and trusted him. In those days this country was largely settled by Presbyterians and Baptists and Quakers—by people with ideas of their own, ways of their own—but like most Virginians they enjoyed attending court. Some times on Court Days whole families drove to the courthouse. They picnicked on the green, gossiped with neighbors, winked at the young bucks trying to hold hands with the girls. Court Days were fun, a change.

When Patrick Henry arose in a courtroom, a ripple of excitement went through the crowd. Those long fingers that were so good on the fiddle strings had a way of catching every pair of eyes and focusing attention on Patrick. Somehow he didn't seem to speak with the tongue, but with the heart. One moment, making a point, his voice would thunder with anger and the next sound as sweet as a child's whisper. One moment the greased pigtail swirled around his head and the next he stood perfectly still, an imposing figure of wise and solemn tranquillity.

Perhaps Patrick knew very little about the law, but he understood people the way a clockmaker understands the mechanics of a watch. In one case the opposing attorney tried to bar "plain farmers" from a jury. Up jumped Patrick, spoiling for a fight. What was wrong with "plain farmers?" Weren't they fair-minded, honest, respectable? Plain farmers decided that Patrick Henry was the man they wanted to send down to Williamsburg to represent them in the House of Burgesses.

Father explained the Stamp Act that so angered the American colonies in 1765. We have all sorts of stamp taxes today and never give them a second thought. There is a stamp tax on the tobacco Father smokes, and on the cards Jane and I use to play rummy, and on many other things. But our representatives in Congress make these taxes, and so we feel responsible for them.

The Stamp Act of 1765 was altogether different in this respect. What made the colonists so mad was the fact that whenever they drew up a legal document like a deed or will, or executed commercial papers like bills and receipts, or bought articles like playing cards, dice, almanacs, pamphlets and newspapers, members of the British Parliament three thousand miles across the sea had decided they must pay a stamp tax. Sometimes the tax was only half a penny and sometimes as much as twenty shillings sterling, but more infuriating than the amount was the high-handed manner in which the taxes were being imposed.

From the beginning influential Virginians had opposed the *idea* of the Stamp Act. If George Wythe liked a light breakfast, his appetite could be even slighter thinking of what these taxes really meant. Easy-going Peyton Randolph, another prominent leader in the House of Burgesses, had no love for the Stamp Act. Old Richard Bland, who had studied the laws so long that some declared his skin had grown to resemble the parchment he was forever handling, frowned and looked even more dried out whenever the taxes were mentioned.

"These men," Father said, "represented the real leaders of the House of Burgesses. They were men of wealth, of position, of long and faithful service to Virginia. Yet now that the Stamp Act had become virtually a *law*, they felt that it must be accepted. And there, of course, is where they differed with Patrick Henry, who had no great awe of these conservative, established leaders. 'The Tidewater crowd,' he might have called them secretly. Did they think they owned all of Virginia—meaning, in Patrick's mind, how Virginians thought and felt and believed?"

So Patrick rode into Williamsburg on his lean, sorrel horse
that bright May day in 1765. Down Duke of Gloucester
Street, past Market Square, the shops, the taverns, the fine
carriages, the walks filled with ladies in silks and gentlemen
in ruffled shirts jogged back-country Patrick. His head was
held high, with a kind of defiant pride befitting the son of a
region where the people pushed back the wilderness with
their own hands, and sometimes almost starved trying to
run crossroads stores, and felt their hackles rising when plain
farmers were challenged as jurymen.

Patrick waited three days before he made his first speech in the House of Burgesses. A number of the Tidewater members, believing that the business of the spring session was about finished and dreading the hot, muggy weather that would come soon enough, already had departed on their long journeys home. Patrick arose, flexing his fingers, fixing his shrewd, dark eyes on John Robinson, the Speaker of the House. He understood, Patrick said, that in order to relieve a money shortage in the colony the establishment of a public loan office had been proposed. Patrick was opposed to the idea. He hoped it would be dropped. In so far as Speaker Robinson had suggested the public loan office, Patrick left no doubt that he wasn't afraid of the old leadership.

So the warning was sounded. Six days passed. The weariest sort of routine occupied the House of Burgesses on May 29 —approving bills for payment. Drowsiness deepened among the legislators when later a bill affecting the militia was read.

Then came the thunderclap. A resolution was offered to debate what steps should be taken as a result of the Stamp Act. Patrick Henry was on his feet in an instant. He would second that motion.

There were no sleepy heads now. The same sense of drama, of excitement that drew the country people to hear Patrick on Court Days spread through the House of Burgesses. Bland glanced at Randolph, Peyton Randolph at George Wythe. Did they, even then, sense the danger that Patrick represented? From a pocket of his jacket, the lawyer in the greased pigtail drew a sheet of paper. He had prepared, he announced, some resolutions *against* the Stamp Act.

And so, stubbornly, willfully, Patrick Henry led Virginia

to a crossroads. One way led to placid obedience, the other to protest, rebellion, unrest and—Revolution?

Resolution after resolution left no doubt of what Patrick Henry was doing. By the time he reached the fifth and final resolution the air in the Capitol chamber seemed charged with the electricity that Benjamin Franklin had captured with a kite string.

Patrick's voice didn't waver. There he stood, proud, defiant, opening and closing those long fingers. Only the General Assembly of Virginia, he cried, had the right to tax the people. If any other body attempted to wrest such power, he shouted, they tended to destroy British as well as American freedom.

The old leadership in the House of Burgesses rallied and managed to put off until the following day consideration of Patrick Henry's resolutions. The session broke up, and the members of the House went out into the May sunlight, doubtless surprised to discover that the spring day remained beautiful and calm here on the green. And then the babel of voices began. Patrick was a hero. Patrick was a headstrong, dangerous scamp.

That was Patrick's greatest gift. He could reach people, getting under their skin, touching their hearts, stirring their minds. Hearing about those resolutions, young Thomas Jefferson knew where he would be next morning—at the Capitol, listening when Patrick resumed speaking. And so Williamsburg slumbered restlessly and awoke next morning to a day that would have lasting meaning to our country.

CHAPTER SIX

A Day Tom Jefferson
Remembered

AT THE EASTERN END of Duke of Gloucester Street
the sun shone brilliantly on the white cupola of the
Capitol. Britain's Flag of the Great Union fluttered
in a freshening breeze. Along this street on that May morning
in 1765 Tom Jefferson's long, impatient strides seemed to
explode like the ideas in his restless mind.

Tom wanted to hear Patrick Henry defend those resolutions. Clearly, Patrick was one of those keyed-up fellows,
high-spirited, like a horse that tried to seize the bit and run.
Sooner or later, if a frisky horse wasn't controlled, he upset
the carriage.

A growing excitement nudged Jefferson toward the Capitol. Now twenty-two, Tom had grown into a thin-boned
chap who, in mind and body, sometimes seemed stretched
as taut as a fiddle string. With Tom, allowance always had
to be made for the reddish tint of his hair. Underneath, he
was a great deal like Patrick Henry, possessing a fighter's in-
stinct. Tom knew that compared to the wealth of the Tidewater planters who controlled the House of Burgesses, Patrick
was a penniless upstart. But there was another sort of riches

that Jefferson always understood—riches of ideas, of determination to get ahead, of faith in one's self.

Jefferson had lived almost five years in Williamsburg, and, hurrying along Duke of Gloucester Street, the town now seemed as familiar as a comfortable old shoe. Even the shops and taverns had become old friends, a part of Tom. The barber and peruke-maker, in the building next to the King's Arms Tavern, shaved him for a penny and made the tie wig that, with the devil's luck, still sat straight on Tom's head.

Without looking, young Jefferson guessed that the bust of Sit Walter Raleigh continued to gaze down in solemn perplexity from its perch above the doorway to Raleigh Tavern. After all, there existed a limit to how far Patrick Henry could go in disrupting the town! Behind the tavern at this very moment the bread *had* to be in the brick oven of the bake shop—and, considering the nature of the fellow, the baker *had* to be seated on his doorstep puffing on a clay pipe and sunning himself.

Farther down the street, Tom passed Doctor Galt's Apothecary Shop. Just yesterday Tom had bought a five-penny twig, taking the doctor's word that it would make a fine wintergreen toothbrush. When Tom had entered the shop, he had interrupted Galt in the serious business of whetting a knife blade on the sole of his shoe.

"An operation this morning?" Tom had asked, for Galt also served Williamsburg as surgeon and dentist.

The doctor had nodded. Doubtless, if Tom wanted to try the European method of relieving a headache, Doctor Galt would bore a hole in his head to let out the hot air and vapors. Tom could think of better ways of becoming open-minded.

From the Apothecary Shop to the Capitol Jefferson's spindly legs could cover the distance in a few strides. The human beehive that Williamsburg became during Public Times had its center at the grounds surrounding this H-shaped building. Merchants, ship captains, tobacco planters congregated here, transacting the "money business" of the colony in the good fresh air, and putting aside local pride and confessing that toward late spring it could get hot as blazes in Virginia. Frontiersmen in buckskin breeches, an occasional Indian in beaded jacket and moccasins, members of the House of Burgesses in velvet suits and satin waistcoats all could be found strolling the grounds.

No one knew the true Virginia until he had seen the Capitol grounds during Public Times. There was something in the air then that made the blood tingle. No one could touch this substance—it wasn't, after all, anything you could hold in the hand like the horehound drops Doctor Galt sold—and yet it was as sweet when the imagination tasted it. That was the magical quality of Public Times—this sense of understanding and believing and reaching decisions because levelheaded men trusted in themselves. Independence wasn't anything more than an individual's willingness to be self sufficient, to look out for himself. And to look out for others also, only that trait was called self-government.

Tom Jefferson was a good student of the history of Virginia. This spirit of self-reliance had been part of the colony even in 1607, when the first Englishmen had settled on the sandy soil of Jamestown. Some ninety years later, when the capital had been moved inland to Williamsburg, that spirit had moved right along. It was almost as though those first

settlers had uncorked a bottle, and a kind of headstrong genie
had escaped and would forever defy recapture.

"Father's swiping his ideas from the Arabian Nights
Tales," I said.

"I like it," Jane said. "Why can't there be a Virginian genie
as well as an Arabian one? Why do they have to own all the
magic?"

"After all," Father reasoned, "liberty is a spirit. You can
feel it but you can't see it."

So we decided to let Father have his genie in Virginia, a
sort of wayward fellow who sneaked around stirring up a
feeling of independence. Father, pleased at this concession,
returned to Jefferson that May morning looking across the
green to the Capitol. What Tom saw was a building composed of two wings connected by a center hall. In one wing
sat the Council, appointed by the King himself. A handsome
turkey work carpet covered the table of this chamber. Chairs,
tables, even the inkpots and candlesticks were products of
fine craftsmanship. The walls were beautifully paneled.

In contrast, the other wing seemed as plain as a pin. Here
sat the House of Burgesses, elected by the people. Simple
cushioned wooden benches lined the walls of this meeting-
room. A back-country Patrick Henry could never blurt out
defiance of Parliament and the Stamp Act in the Council, but
in the House of Burgesses—well, there was the difference.

That late May morning found a crowd gathered in the
lobby facing the room where the Burgesses met. Jefferson,
squeezing into a space by the door, could say long legs and
bony elbows held some advantage. Many places on the

benches were unoccupied, and, for all the session had accomplished thus far, no one could blame those who had made an early start home. A dreary debate over a disputed election in one of the counties was followed by another over a bill to regulate Indian trade.

Sunlight came through the windows. Tom's friend and tutor, George Wythe, lifted a pinch of snuff to his nose, then sneezed rather violently. Restless lawmakers stretched their legs, leaned over the benches, whispered—in a way, they were like schoolboys chafing at a class that promised never to end. Patrick Henry's greased pigtail and homespun clothes could be quickly spotted among the velvets and satins of his bewigged comrades. Many eyes followed Patrick—appraising him, wondering. He looked calm, resolute, a fellow who wouldn't scare easily.

At last portly Peyton Randolph arose, looking as though he had never wasted a crumb of those twelve-course dinners served at Raleigh Tavern. Usually the most affable man in Williamsburg, today Peyton Randolph seemed serious, reserved, cautious in both his double chins. In Randolph's hand were the five resolutions Patrick had offered. Their intention, their danger were clear enough to him.

Yet Patrick, standing up to speak in behalf of his resolutions, still possessed that cool look. Jefferson, listening intently, caught here and there a slip in grammar. With Patrick, such awkwardness didn't matter. His words flowed on, majestic in their sweep, important because of the man behind them. Poor Tom, whose own voice was high-pitched and raspy, caught the spell of Patrick. As long as Jefferson lived, he would remember this speech. In the spring, after a cloudburst,

a brook rushing down a hill lifted mighty obstacles and carried them along like dried reeds. That strength was in the
voice of the Son of Thunder.

A glance around the room revealed troubled, sober faces.
Wythe's, for one. Peyton Randolph's, for another. A pinched
scowl settled between the dark eyes of Speaker Robinson.
Richard Bland looked down at his ruffled shirt. The thoughts
of these men weren't difficult to imagine. The old leadership
of the House of Burgesses, which they represented, was being
challenged by this new kind of Virginian, this new kind of
independence.

Yet no one could deny that Patrick Henry was winning the day. Resolution after resolution was put to a vote. Sober faces, taut nerves, thin-edged tempers didn't seem to change the result. Each time Patrick came out on top—even carrying the fiery fifth resolution that declared only the General Assembly had the right to levy taxes, although his margin of victory had dwindled by then to a single vote.

Jefferson stood in the lobby where Peyton Randolph strode from the room.

"Five hundred guineas," Randolph muttered. He would have given this sum gladly for a single vote, so that the balloting on the fifth resolution would have ended in a tie and Speaker Robinson could have cast the deciding vote against Henry!

Once the Son of Thunder blundered. Swept away by his own oratory, he cried:"Caesar had his Brutus, Charles the First his Cromwell, and George the Third—" Speaker Robinson spoke sharply. This was threatening the King. This was treason. Afterward the story went around that Patrick Henry flared back:"If this be treason, make the most of it!"

But the story is no longer believed. More likely, Patrick apologized for any offense he had given and there the matter ended. Patrick might be one of "the young hot and giddy members"who Governor Fauquier complained had wormed their way into the House of Burgesses, but he was no fool. Rather, he seemed just the opposite—a chap who looked before he leaped and knew exactly where he intended to land.

Jane liked Patrick Henry."I'm glad he got the better of the old worry-warts," she declared.

"Did he, though?"

"Well, you just said—"

Father grinned. Jane might as well learn now, he said, that at times politics can be a slippery game. After Patrick and one or two of his supporters had left town, Speaker Robinson and Peyton Randolph talked long and earnestly to some of the more conservative members. A motion was offered—and carried—to strike the fifth resolution from the record of the session!

Yet, in a sense, Robinson and Randolph succeeded simply in bolting the stable door after the horse had escaped. News of Patrick Henry's speech and resolutions apparently traveled wherever the breeze blew across Virginia. People talked about the Son of Thunder, nodded their heads, and acted pleased that someone at last had spoken out, straight from the shoulder. The Stamp Act was like a nettle under their skins. And, like Patrick, there were a great many more of this new kind of Virginian in the making than some of the conservatives in Williamsburg suspected.

Actually, a new kind of American was in the making. Within a very short time he also knew about Henry's defiance, and the story grew better as imagination enlarged it. In Rhode Island and Massachusetts newspapers claimed one of the Virginian's resolutions had declared that anyone who asserted the right of taxation did not rest exclusively with the General Assembly became "an enemy to his Majesty's colony!"

"Oh! Those Virginians are men!" cried one Bostonian.

So the story of Patrick Henry's revolt—the true story and the made-up one—roused colonists everywhere to thrust out belligerent chins at mention of the Stamp Act. A seed had been planted. By mid-autumn its roots were reaching out.

We went into the Capitol and stood by the door, looking into the chamber of the House of Burgesses where Patrick Henry had sown this first seed of revolution. On the table stood the wooden ballot box, the symbol of free men. The high-backed speaker's chair looked down on the wooden benches around the wall. Jane said that she expected to hear the rustle of velvets and satins at any moment and to see the old patriots march through the door—Wythe and Peyton Randolph and Patrick Henry.

Father nodded. But his story wasn't finished. There was rather an exciting sequel, he told us, beginning on October 30th, two days before the Stamp Act was due to become law, when George Mercer reached Williamsburg. The town was again crowded, for the General Court was in session. Mercer's coming had been talked about—he was the distributor of stamps for Virginia. In the taverns, in the coffee houses, anger underscored almost every comment about this tax. In a surly mood, a group from the taverns and coffee houses decided to meet Mr. Mercer. They found him at the steps of the Capitol.

Almost a mob spirit ruled the men confronting Virginia's distributor of stamps. They meant business—even a bit of rough, ugly business, if necessary. Questions were flung at young Mercer. Was he going to try to collect that tax? Or would he have the good sense to resign his office?

George Mercer hedged, a nice young fellow of good Virginian background. He needed time to think. By Friday morning at ten o'clock he would tell these gentlemen what he intended to do.

That answer satisfied no one. By Friday the Stamp Act would have become law.

Mercer sought refuge in the coffee house across from the Capitol. Muttering, unruly, the crowd trailed after him, filling the road outside. Both Mercer's father and brother were lawyers who had come to Williamsburg to attend the session of the General Court. They didn't hide their concern.

"I've got a duty to discharge," Mercer said, his dander rising.

"You've got a neck to save," they told him.

Outside the grumbles grew louder. Anger bred impatience. From time to time messengers appeared in the coffee house. Mercer must make up his mind by not later than tomorrow. But Mercer had meant what he said. They would have his answer on Friday. Again no one was satisfied and now a new cry was raised:

"Let us rush in!"

With Mercer at the coffee house that evening was Governor Fauquier, a man of sound sense. This situation could easily get out of hand. Fauquier believed that, generally, the people of the colony liked him. He was the spunky sort, anyhow—not seeking a fight but not backing down before the prospect of one. Fauquier came out on the porch, facing the crowd. A new shout greeted him:

"See the Governor. Take care of him."

Fauquier stood his ground, a bit bull-doggish, after the British pattern. He spoke quietly. He had extracted a promise from Mercer, he said, to give the people an answer if they would meet him at the Capitol at five o'clock tomorrow evening. Now it was growing dark and the Governor wished

to go home. Moreover he had asked Mercer to accompany
him.

The crowd parted, somewhat grudgingly, to make a path.
Some angry mutters were heard. All right, others grumbled,
they would wait until tomorrow evening. A kind of threatening undertone rumbled in these voices.

At five o'clock next afternoon the crowd reformed at the
Capitol. Poor Mercer had lived through a miserable night
and day. He had consulted with Fauquier, and talked again

with his father and brother, who, in the Governor's estimate, "were both frightened out of their senses." Mercer faced the stolid Virginians. His announcement was brief. He would resign his office.

All at once the crowd erupted with cheers. Good for Mercer! He had stood with the colony after all! That night taverns overflowed with gay celebrants. Drums beat out a happy cadence. Wherever one looked the houses of Williamsburg seemed to glow with lights. The new kind of Virginian felt proud of his new kind of independence. Afterward when those Williamsburg people learned of the riots in Boston and Newport, Wilmington and New York, that had marked the opposition to the Stamp Act, they slapped one another on the back, congratulating themselves on how much more sensibly they had handled the same situation.

"But what if Mercer hadn't resigned?" Jane asked.

"Oh, don't go borrowing trouble," Father said.

As events developed in only a few years, maybe Father was right about the genie. That fellow, now that he was out of his bottle, soon seemed to be breathing mischief at every turn—that is, if you took the other point of view. Patrick Henry certainly had felt the genie's bite, or heard his whisper, or whatever was the way he went about working his spell. And Tom Jefferson was pretty much the genie's victim already, and Washington never had been afraid of anything —the Ohio wilderness or an idea.

But even the more conservative leaders, so dead set against Patrick in 1765, would change—not all at once, but gradually, irresistibly. By 1770 no one could mistake the difference.

CHAPTER SEVEN

"The Dye Is Now Cast"

SPRING CREPT SLOWLY up the Virginia Peninsula. In the gardens the tulips pushed sturdy green stalks through the ground and leaves unfurled on the willow and elm, the mulberry and sycamore trees. In the dawn, dashing out for that cold shower, George Wythe saw impudent robins staring at his jigs and splashes, and Tom Jefferson, working on his law cases, heard the piercing whistle of the cardinals.

June of 1770 brought Washington to Williamsburg. In his eleventh year now as a member of the House of Burgesses, the squire of Mount Vernon stayed by custom at a lodging house. The brief daily entries in Washington's diary revealed a man of steady habits and quiet industry:

9. *Had a cold Cut at Mrs. Campbell's and went up to Eltham in the afternoon.*

11. *Went over to Colo. Thos. Moore's Sale and purchased two Negroes, to wit Frank and James, and returned to Eltham again at night.*

14. *Dined at the Speaker's and went to Bed by 8 Oclock.*

18. *Came into Williamsburg in the morning. Dined at the Club and went to the Play in the afternoon.*

19. *Dined at the Club and went to the Play.*

20. *Dined at the President's and went to the Play afterwards.*

Next day Washington supped at Mrs. Campbell's and was in bed by eight—a big man, propped against the pillows, sleeping in a half sitting-up position as was the custom in those days—but an afternoon later he returned to his seat in the theatre, looking up at the crude stage and following with enchantment every spoken line, every move of the unfolding drama.

Williamsburg's theatre stood on the edge of the forest, and performers who could handle a gun had no reason to starve—they could stand in the door and bag a turkey or duck or a rabbit for a stew. Yet a steady playgoer like Washington was a greater boon to their appetites. Once they saw him in the audience five successive performances, a tribute to red-headed Nancy Hallam, the favorite actress of the period. Between acts, while the scenery was being shifted, magicians, jugglers and trapeze artists often kept the audience entertained.

But more than red-headed actresses, magicians and jugglers kept tongues wagging in Williamsburg those outwardly peaceful weeks in 1770. On a raw March day in Boston snowballs had been hurled at a British sentry and shots had been fired at the howling, derisive crowd. Three civilians had been killed, eight wounded and ship captains, reaching Williamsburg that spring, brought copies of an engraving of the "Boston Massacre." A silversmith named Paul Revere had set his hand to making this record of the brutal scene. He had intended that, beholding it, eyes should snap and tempers flare.

Up the street from the Capitol stood Raleigh Tavern. Here
the spring before the Boston Massacre occurred another event
that had revealed how deeply, in only four years, the roots

were spreading from the seed of revolution planted by Patrick Henry. The day was May 17, 1769, when Washington, his face lined with sober purpose, crossed Duke of Gloucester Street and mounted the steps of the inn.

Noisy planters, merchants, lawyers and students from the college crowded the taproom to the left of the main hallway. Serving boys trotted from table to table with tankards of ale, measured in pints and quarts so that there was sound logic to the expression advising the prudent man to watch his p's and q's. A pipe smoker called for the Honor Box, inserted his penny in the slot, and smiled at the friend who watched owlishly to make certain that he took no more than the single pipe bowl of tobacco the penny covered.

The gaming tables, usually busy, seemed to have lost their interest. Watching the hall a planter said, "There's Washington."

Another said: "That's Charles Carter from Lancaster. And there's Burwell Basset."

"There's Thomas Jefferson," still a third added. "And George Wythe."

A fourth planter, piecing the puzzle together, exclaimed: "The members of the House of Burgesses are assembling here. What trouble is underway now?"

The Burgesses made their way down the hall to the Apollo Room. Often they had come here in gay spirits to attend a dance or dinner, but today the motto above the mantelpiece in the Apollo Room did not reflect their feelings. In Latin that motto read, "Hilaritas Sapientiae et Bonae Vitae Proles," and in English meant, "Jollity, the offspring of wisdom and good living." "Wisdom" the Burgesses believed they still possessed, or otherwise they would not be here. "Good living" they certainly wanted, and upon that precise point rested their present grievance with the new Governor of the colony, Lord Botetourt (his name was pronounced "Bottitott"). As for "Jollity" — they could only hope that time would restore that.

It was not long before those in the taproom of the Raleigh learned what was behind the meeting in the Apollo Room.

"Ye heard?" merchant asked friend. "Governor Botetourt called the Burgesses into the chamber of the Council and dissolved them—or sent them home, so to speak, with their tails between their legs! It was all because of the resolves they adopted on May 16 and the address to the King in protest against prisoners taken in America being transported to England for trial."

"An unfair business," the friend said bitterly. "What sort of justice is that? Or will a prisoner's witnesses be transported with him so he can stand a fair trial?"

"You know they will not, unless the poor devil can foot the bill himself."

Ale loosened tongues. Wise heads in the taproom knew that this grievance was only one of many, a symptom of a kind of illness spreading throughout British America. After the Stamp Act had been repealed along had come the Townshend Acts placing duties on the import of glass, lead, paint, paper and tea.

"A lot of grit gets stuck in the same chicken's crop," a planter said.

How shrewd this observation would prove was revealed next day by the agreements reached in the Apollo Room by the Burgesses, who called themselves "his Majesty's most dutiful subjects, the late Representatives of all the Freeholders of the Colony of Virginia."

With the exception of paper, the Burgesses declared, they would import no article of merchandise or manufacture that was taxed by Parliament for the purpose of raising a revenue in America. A long list was made of specific articles that would not be imported if so taxed, including beef, pork and fish, watches, clocks and looking glasses, hats, shoes and boots. Until the taxes were withdrawn, the men in the Apollo Room pledged that after the first day of November they would not import any slave or purchase any imported slave. After the first of September wines of any kind were placed under the same ban. Further,"his Majesty's most dutiful subjects"agreed:

"For the better Preservation of the Breed of Sheep, That they will not kill, or suffer to be killed, any Lambs, that shall be weaned before the First Day of May, in any Year, nor dispose of such to any Butcher or other Person, whom they may have Reason to expect, intends to kill the same."

Pleased with this work, the wine was brought in and toasts drunk to the King, to the Queen and royal family, to Lord Botetourt and prosperity to Virginia, to a speedy and lasting Union between Great Britain and her colonies, and to "the constitutional British Liberty in America, and all true Patriots, the Supporters thereof."

But now another year had passed, and looking at Paul Revere's engraving citizens of Williamsburg saw how British troops, firing on a Boston crowd, had killed three and wounded eight. Thoughtful men slept uneasily.

Yet the days still were much the same for Peter at the silversmith's shop, and for Anne when she walked down Duke of Gloucester Street with her market basket, and for Eliza in her shoe-fly chair mumbling to herself as she pretended that she could read the *Virginia Gazette*. For young John, the scrawny lad who worked at the *Gazette's* office, there remained ink smears to wash off his face, or the same collection of poor devils to behold in pillory or the stocks before the Public Gaol on Nicholson Street.

John felt somewhat shamefaced afterward, remembering how one day he had thrown an overripe tomato at one unfortunate fellow who was in the stocks for failing to mind his p's and q's. It was punishment enough just to be thrown into that forbidding hole of a gaol without being pegged with rotten vegetables or hooted at by passersby. Once Peter Oldham, the jailer, had let John see inside the cells and shivers still ran down the boy's spine at the memory of the leg irons and wall chains, the smelly straw on the floor that was the only bed a prisoner had no matter how cold and damp the nights became, the little slot in the thick wall through which the prisoner received his sparse meal of "salt beef damaged, and Indian meal."

Well, John thought, that place put a chap in a mind to think twice before he acted the villain. On the other hand, a man who owed money wasn't necessarily a rascal—he was just broke. But debtors found themselves jailed unless friends or members of their families paid off their obligations, or the court eventually took mercy on them.

John hoped he would never be a fool and become a debtor. And he guessed he'd walk a straight line, considering that

along with imprisonment could go a fine, lashing, and even mutilation. Or a stout rope around your neck if convicted of arson, piracy, horse stealing, forgery or burglary, since all these crimes could be punished by hanging.

The boy had heard about those thirteen pirates, henchmen of the notorious Blackbeard, who had been hanged in Williamsburg. It made no difference to John that these executions

had taken place in 1718, almost forty years before John had
been born. Every time he passed the Public Gaol he thought
of those thirteen corpses stretched in a row—sometimes he
imagined that the pock-marked pirate in the middle possessed a wooden leg with a skull and crossbones carved into
the side of it!

But even such attractive horrors of the imagination as
dangling pirates couldn't compare to the actual delights of
the Fair in April or December. Then, ogling at a poster tacked
to a tree on Market Square, John's heartbeat quickened as
he read:

"A saddle of 40s. value, to be run for, once around the
Mile Course, adjacent to this City, by any Horse, Mare or
Gelding, carrying Horseman's Weight, and allowing weight
for inches. A handsome bridle to be given to the horse that
comes in second. And a good whip to the horse that comes
in third."

Or:

"A Pair of Silver Buckles, value 20s. to be run for by Men,
from the College to the Capitol. A Pair of Shoes to be given
to him that comes in second. And a Pair of Gloves to the
third."

Or:

"A Pig, with his Tail soap'd, to be run after; and to be
given to the Person that catches him, and lifts him off the
Ground fairly by the Tail."

Usually the Fair lasted three days. Prizes were given to the
person who brought the best draught horse for sale, or to the
person who brought the most cows, steers "or other horned
cattle." So much to see, so much to do—*there*, John spied a

sentence on the poster that he had missed at first glance: "A Pair of Pumps to be danc'd for by Men."

The betting at the horse races was lively, and it made little difference that there was not much "hard money" in the colony, and that what little there was became so prudently used that a coin worth fifty cents would be cut into four pieces or "bits" for easier exchange. Anyhow, one could bet without money. "I'll wager you one pistol to two," shouted the backer of one horse to another.

"My mare's the best," the other cried, "and to prove it I'll put up a cow and a calf to any hog that you've got!"

Whether a horse race was more exciting than a wrestling match, young John couldn't say. You could always spot the fellows who expected to fight, for they let their fingernails grow long. Virginia rules for wrestling were catch as catch can—a match could become a hair-raiser to watch, both literally and figuratively.

Rarely was there better dancing anywhere than during a Fair—twenty fiddlers sawing away at once, heels kicking in the country jigs. There were concerts, singing contests, and one year a fellow named Joseph Faulks could be seen "riding one, two, and three horses, in many different attitudes"—perhaps a performance that qualified as the grandfather of the Wild West Show in America!

Still, as the months went by, the arrival of ship captains or the post riders with newspapers from the other colonies brought news of an unrest spreading through British America. In June of 1772 a strange affair occurred in the harbor off Providence, Rhode Island. There were now in New England hot-heads called "Separatists," and no one knew how far they would go in opposing the authority of the British crown. When one afternoon His Majesty's armed schooner *Gaspée* arrived off Providence its mission was to try to catch some local smugglers. The *Gaspée*, however, ran aground and that night several boatloads of men put out from shore. Soon startling news raced through the colonies—the *Gaspée* had been burned, her crew"captured"!

Much depended on how deeply one had been angered by the Stamp Act and the Townshend Acts, among other measures, in determining how one judged the *Gaspée* affair. Many held the raiders to be heroes, others deplored any form of violence, and of course in England there was only one cry—this was out and out piracy.

On both sides of the Atlantic necks were growing redder, backs bristling, tempers simmering. The meeting in 1769 in the Apollo Room of Raleigh Tavern, and similar action in other colonies, had won in time repeal of the Townshend Acts. But King George III had his stubborn streak. He insisted that a duty must be kept on tea, saying,"The dye is now cast, the Colonies must either submit or triumph; I do not wish to come to severer measures but we must not retreat . . . there must always be one tax to keep up the right, and as such I approve the Tea Duty."

The Boston Tea Party followed, and in retaliation Parliament ordered the port of Boston closed beginning June 1, 1774. That day would not soon be forgotten in Williamsburg.

For George Wythe not even his eggs, toast and coffee followed the cold shower that morning. Anne and Peter also went without breakfast, and the baker at Raleigh Tavern doubted if he should even fire his oven. Across the street at his lodging house, Washington looked out at the morning sunlight and remembered, "I must go to church today."

Thomas Jefferson awakened to mingled emotions. He was a married man now, with a fine new home rising on his beloved mountain top at Charlottesville. The long journeys to Williamsburg were harder to bear, even with the comfort of a small violin he carried with him so that he could amuse himself along the way by fiddling a tune. Yet few events aroused Jefferson as the closing of the port of Boston, or made him more determined to have his influence felt in Williamsburg.

"What has the King done?" Jefferson asked his friend in the House of Burgesses, Robert Carter Nicholas. Because the people in Boston refused to pay a tax on tea, they were being stripped of their liberty. Boston seemed a long way from Virginia, and doubtless that was why the King believed this act could be risked—what cared the other colonies what happened in one?

"But we do care," Jefferson said. That was why he wished Nicholas to introduce a resolution whereby, in sympathy for the unjust treatment to the people of Boston, June first would become a day of prayer and fasting in Virginia. If the people of Boston thus could be enslaved, then might not Virginians be next if it should please the King's fancy? For a long time a thought had been growing in Jefferson's mind that fitted well the spirit of his revolt now: "It is God who gave us life and God who gave us liberty!"

The resolution that Jefferson proposed to Nicholas passed easily. On June first the doors of Bruton Church stood open.

Here many persons, like Washington, like Anne and Peter
and Johnny the printer's apprentice, came to pray for the
afflictions of their fellow colonists in Massachusetts. They
believed, as Jefferson once said, "The King's argument is with
God—not with us."

"Old Bruton Parish Church," Father said, relishing the
sound of the words.

When we entered this old building at the corner of Duke of
Gloucester Street and Palace Green, Jane fell into what Father
calls her Sunday habit, for whenever she enters a church she
walks on the tips of her toes—expecting, I suppose, to ascend
into heaven at any moment.

The stone font was brought from Jamestown, and was
used when Washington stood as godfather at the baptism of
fourteen slaves. Originally an outside stairway provided a
separate entrance to the north transept gallery, where the
slaves sat. They, too, watched in Bruton Church on that day
of fasting, humiliation and prayer when all the members of
the House of Burgesses came in a body "to implore the divine
interposition, for averting the heavy Calamity which threatens destruction to our Civil Rights, and the Evils of civil
War."

As Washington, Peyton Randolph, Wythe and Robert
Carter Nicholas arrived with the Burgesses to pray in Bruton
Church, sunlight filtered through the arched windows and
cast a soft glow over chancel and nave. The large square pew,
set aside for the Governor and his twelve councilors, with a
canopied chair where the Governor sat, was empty this day.
The transept pews were reserved for the Burgesses, the pews
in the west gallery for the students from William and Mary.

Peter Pelham, the town jailor, played the organ—assisted by a prisoner, whom he always brought along to do the hard work of pumping.

Likely after services at Bruton, homeward-bound worshippers had their own opinion of the organ playing. Perhaps

they grumbled,"We need to jail some scoundrel who can pump with more godly vigor!"

Sometimes in books history can seem remote, something that belonged to a few great men and women, but back at the roots of the stuff, where you can feel it growing around you, all sorts of people become important. Peter Pelham played his organ, and a prisoner pumped, and the Burgesses came to pray, and the silversmith locked the door under the Sign of the Golden Ball to follow the procession down Duke of Gloucester Street, and Johnny's face was scrubbed clean of ink smears earlier in the day than it had been for weeks, and the ovens cooled in the baker's kitchen—that was history as people lived it, in their hearts and with their minds and hands.

Jane remembered Father's genie. "That rascal was beginning to infect a lot of people," she said with a laugh.

"And none more deeply than Jefferson," Father agreed. "Before 1774 ended everywhere in the colonies—and in England too—the power of his pen would be recognized. Really this was the year when Jefferson, as the future author of the Declaration of Independence, experienced a 'new birth of life'."

It might seem a strange circumstance, Father said, but he'd wager that one of the first places where this fact had been truly understood was in the print shop where young Johnny tormented himself with images of those thirteen pirates stretched in a row.

CHAPTER EIGHT

The Devil's Tail

W HEN JOHNNY JARRATT was only seven, he made the long journey with his father to deliver a roasting pig to the tavern at New Kent Courthouse. Never had Johnny felt more puffed out with importance. His mother looked at the lad, mounted on the old sway-backed horse, and thought how much like a pin he seemed—really more head than body.

"'Tis your first trip away from home," the woman said, flustered and saddened at the thought. "There and back, 'tis a powerful ways for a young sprite like you."

"I'll be keeping my eye on the child," Johnny's father said, rather crossly, "Or do you think I'll let him drown crossing the Pamunkey River on the ferry?"

"If it's very much ale you take to drinking, he'll be the one who will do the watching," Mrs. Jarratt flung back, in no mood to take a rebuke from a mere husband. She was filled with last minute advice for Johnny:

"Mind your manners, boy. Along the river you'll see fine plantation homes where the people drink coffee and tea just as freely as we'd drink water. Use your eyes but hold your tongue, for 'tis no credit to ask foolish questions of those who are your betters. Some day you may need their favor, so let the impression you make be good!"

"You'd think already we were setting off to find Johnny a place as an apprentice in Williamsburg," the father grumbled. "You'll have years to scheme over that yet, woman, so let us get this day's journey over first!"

Johnny's head whirled with thoughts of the adventure before him, and also with the first inkling he ever had gleaned of the plans his parents had of some day sending him off to Williamsburg.

"In another two or three years we'll talk about that," Mr. Jarratt said after they had started, and his broad Irish face seemed to turn red when the sunlight brought out the deep tint of his whiskers. "It's not much, grubbing on a backwoods farm the way we do—not for a lad with a full life ahead of him. You can learn a trade and do better, which is what a man really wants—to see his son do the things he might like to have accomplished himself. Who knows, the day might come, Johnny, when you'll get used to the taste of tea and coffee!"

Johnny nodded eagerly. This was the longest speech except one that he ever had heard his father make, and since the other speech had been addressed to a pig that escaped down a brook one day with his father in angry pursuit, the first occasion was perhaps better forgotten.

Tobacco fields where Negro slaves worked under the scrutiny of an overseer mounted on a horse gave Johnny his first glimpse into plantation life. No wonder a man grew rich with all those people to help him! Then riding down to Williams' Ferry the boy saw across the river the beautiful mansion of a plantation owner.

"That's Poplar Grove," the ferry keeper told them, "and

its master is Richard Chamberlayne. A heap of important people visit there, including Colonel George Washington. I guess you know that it was at Poplar Grove Colonel Washington met Martha Custis. She's Mrs. Washington now, and right soon she and the Colonel will be waiting just where you are so that the ferry can take them across the river on their way to Williamsburg."

Johnny and his father were delayed at the ferry, for the northern post rider was expected shortly. Still, the elder Jarratt did not mind the wait since the ferry keeper loaned him the latest copy of the *Virginia Gazette*. Now Johnny was glad for all the time his mother had spent teaching him to read for he was able to recognize whole sentences in the paper. The fact that he could read and the fact that there was a *Virginia Gazette* would have special meaning for Johnny in only a few years, and bring him back to Williams' Ferry on the most important journey of his life.

But today his mind was exploding with the visions of a new world opening around him. Crossing the ferry, he sniffed the fresh breeze of the Pamunkey, and, looking more intently at Poplar Grove, was awed to think that just a few people could live in a big mansion like that. In contrast the tavern at New Kent Courthouse seemed rather commonplace, for all that a porch ran across its entire front. And it was the innkeeper's youngsters, Ben and Sally, who led Johnny into his one uncomfortable incident of the entire journey.

The sound of another horse on the road stopped all three children in the game they were playing. When they looked up, they saw the rider, a man of about fifty in a tight if dusty wig.

Sally seized Johnny's arm. "You come with me," she
urged.

"Yes, *git*," Ben prodded, pushing him from behind.

Ben's manner and Sally's communicated a strange sense of
fear to Johnny. Without quite knowing why, he found himself running toward a haystack behind the inn, then crouch-
ing there so that the bewigged rider on the horse couldn't
see him. A tremendous pounding rose in his heart.

"He's a member of the House of Burgesses," Ben said,
almost in a whisper.

"What will he do to us?" Johnny managed to ask at last.

"He won't do nothing," Sally answered decisively, "because he's not going to see us!"

Seven years had passed since that incident, and Johnny,

who was completing his second year as an apprentice in the *Gazette* office, often remembered it. He had grown accustomed to seeing Burgesses in fine clothes and periwigs, and could look them in the eye without feeling his flesh grow pimply. Still, he always wondered how many country children had been frightened by them and had hidden until they were gone.

Johnny had lived in Williamsburg through four Fairs— or two years, for those who reckoned time by the calendar. The pattern of his life in 1774 was easy-going, for all the hard work at the *Gazette* office. Johnny now knew the taste of tea and coffee—and of hot bread from the baker's oven, and horehound drops from Galt's apothecary (he had been given them first the day he fell out of a tree, for horehound was believed to be good for bruises resulting from high falls), and the bitter taste of ale for the proprietor at the Market Square Tavern always greeted Johnny, when he delivered the *Gazette*, with, "Here, laddie, this'll wash off your kidney!" Johnny didn't like the ale, but since cleanliness was next to godliness he didn't see how he could afford to ignore the sanctity of his kidney.

All days were busy in Clementina Rind's print shop. There was no end to the work that went into printing a newspaper, and now of course there was that pamphlet also to set in type and rush through the press. Yesterday Johnny had read the title page: *A Summary View of the Rights of British America. Set Forth in Some Resolutions Intended for the Inspection of the Present Delegates of the People of Virginia. Now in Convention.* The pamphlet was signed, "By a Native, and Member of the House of Burgesses."

"But I know who the author really is," Johnny exclaimed. "'Tis Thomas Jefferson!"

"Aye, 'tis so," Clementina Rind admitted. "Now show me what you know about the work around this shop."

Johnny grinned. In two years he had learned—well, maybe not everything, but almost everything. He had learned how to sort type letters into the boxes known as cases. He had learned how to place and space the letters in a composing stick, and how to tie the type into long columns in a wooden tray called a galley, and how to pound the type flat with a mallet and block so that it would give an even printing surface.

He had learned how to dampen paper to make it more pliable in handling, and how to mix lampblack and varnish to make ink, and how to ink the type with the leather-covered balls. Many long hours he had toiled preparing the dried sheepskin used on those ink balls, suffering valiantly and to the point of losing his appetite forever, since before the pelts could be stretched, they were soaked in a slop pail. Odors there were in life that belonged to the nether region—the odor of a skunk and these dripping pelts!

Treading out pelts was Johnny's principal chore this morning—was it any wonder that he preferred to think of almost anything else? He remembered the words, "Now in Convention."

Hot summer had followed that June day when at Bruton Church the House of Burgesses had fasted and prayed in sympathy for the closing of the port of Boston. Virginia by then had a new Governor, Lord Dunmore, who of course had dissolved the assembly in retaliation for this action against Parliament. So again the Burgesses walked to Raleigh Tavern, eighty-nine of them crowding the Apollo Room. Again they drew up an agreement, and this time there was both a sting and a threat in their recommendations:

"We are further clearly of Opinion that an Attack, made on one of our sister Colonies, to compel submission to arbitrary Taxes, is an Attack make on all British America, and threatens Ruin to the Rights of all, unless the united Wisdom of the Whole be applied. And for this Purpose it is recommended to the Committee of Correspondence, that they communicate, with their several corresponding Committees, on the Expediency of appointing Deputies from the several Colonies of British America, to meet in general Congress, at such Place annually as shall be thought most convenient; there to deliberate on those general Measures which the United Interests of America may from Time to Time require."

A new word, an exciting word appeared twice in that paragraph—the word "united." The colonies possessed a "united wisdom,"and should act in accordance with their "united interests"! There were now committees of correspondence throughout the colonies because one day Jefferson and some of his friends had met secretly at Raleigh Tavern. True, committees on correspondence had been established earlier in Massachusetts, but it remained for Jefferson and his friends in their secret meeting to incite other colonies to similar action. So, really, had the idea of "union" been inspired, and now, in a bolder leap, the idea of a congress representing all the colonies.

During the hot summer days Virginia's leaders assembled in Williamsburg to elect their representatives to the First Continental Congress that would meet in September in Philadelphia. Peyton Randolph, who would have given five hundred guineas a few years before for the vote to defeat Patrick Henry's final resolution against the Stamp Act, now

stood in double-chinned resistance to Parliament, and would become the president of the first Congress. Of course Patrick Henry was another Virginia delegate—a Patrick who hid his greased pigtail under a wig—and so were George Washington, Richard Henry Lee, Richard Bland, Benjamin Harrison, and Edmund Pendleton.

Thomas Jefferson had wanted desperately to attend these

meetings in Williamsburg, but illness confined him to his home at Charlottesville. Jefferson, however, wrote out the ideas he wished to place before the Virginia delegates, and at Peyton Randolph's home on Market Square the document was read aloud.

To men who knew Jefferson, with a mind of his own that couldn't be budged from some ideas by six mules pulling together, the paper may have been no great surprise. Jefferson wrote with fire in his heart, with acid on his pen—no one disputed that. As for what he said—well, they would publish Jefferson's pamphlet and let those who read it decide whether or not they could go along with the zealot on his mountain top!

At Clementina Rind's print shop young Johnny had helped set type on Jefferson's manuscript. Sentences remained in his memory—in a way, they were scorched there. Jefferson listed all the grievances the colonies held toward the King and his Parliament—restrictions that had been placed on trade, the unfair taxes, the suspension in New York of the legislature, the refusal of assent to necessary laws for trifling reasons, dissolution of representative bodies of government for doing their duty, an apparent effort to take from the people the right of representation, the sending of armed troops to the colonies.

"Open your breast Sire, to liberal and expanded thought," Jefferson warned the King. "Let not the name of George the third be a blot in the page of history."

And again:

"The whole art of government consists in the art of being honest."

Johnny gulped. He hadn't believed anybody could dare talk to the King like that! If Ben and Sally hid behind a haystack at the authority represented by a Burgess in his wig, what might they expect if they ever uttered thoughts like these?

"That the sky would fall on their heads," Johnny believed. "And the King's soldiers would impale them on a pitchfork!"

Yet the master printer simply chuckled as his hands, with the swiftness of lightning, plucked the letters from the type case and set other portions of the pamphlet.

"Now, here's an idea for you, Johnny," he called. "Jefferson even blames the King for slavery. He says it wounds the rights of human nature and was forced on us by greedy corsairs at a time when the colonies were too young to resist such an infamous practice."

Correcting proof for mistakes in type-setting, Clementina Rind did not hide her admiration for Jefferson's strong, courageous words. "The god who gave us life," she read, "gave us liberty at the same time; the hand of force may destroy, but cannot disjoin them."

The work of setting type, tying up the pages, locking them in the iron frame so they could be carried to the press advanced steadily. Then the big day came when the printing began. Johnny piled the dampened paper where the master printer could reach it easily. He used the inkballs to spread the ink evenly on the type. Then, when the paper was placed in the right position to print, Johnny seized the long arm of the press—called the devil's tail—and pulled with all his strength. Down came the platen, type and paper met, and Johnny's breath came out in a puff at the hard labor.

"You'll develop a strong right shoulder that way," the master printer remarked cheerfully.

"I suppose it's better to be pulling the devil's tail than being bucked on the seat by his horns," the boy said.

"Aye, that's so," the other agreed, laughing.

Johnny strained once more after another sheet of paper had been placed over the type. He twisted the devil's tail, Johnny said, and Jefferson twisted the King's nose—

"I don't think I'd go too far with that thought," the printer advised, really a prudent man for all the twinkle that danced in his eyes.

"What happened," Jane asked, "when Jefferson's pamphlet was read?"

"Well, the devil had swished his tail for a fact—taking the King's point of view, of course," Father said. Everywhere in the colonies people read *A Summary View* and nodded. There was a sound head on Jefferson's shoulders! Even in England Jefferson suddenly became famous.Maybe he was right, some Britons argued. Why shouldn't Americans decide their own taxes? Was it really right to station troops in the colonies?

A heated debate occupied the British Parliament for hours and resulted in a document known as "Lord North's Proposals." The colonies could decide their own taxes, this document said, but—

"But what?" Jane asked, as though she were one of Jefferson's own daughters and she had stepped back through almost two centuries.

"But the amount of taxes to be raised would be decided in England," Father said.

"That didn't change anything—not so it mattered," Jane snapped. From her stormy face, some mighty slick diplomacy would be necessary to save us from another war with England.

But Jefferson knew this tax proposal was a dodge—and

wrote a hard-headed reply to Lord North. Meanwhile events moved along.

A vessel carrying tea arrived off Yorktown in November of 1774.

And Lady Dunmore, the Governor's wife, had a baby.

And the Governor tried to snitch the colony's supply of gunpowder.

It takes, you see, no end of things to make history work!

CHAPTER NINE

Tea, a Baby, and Gunpowder

PETER WONDERED if he were doing right, and what Anne would say when she learned of the possible mischief in which he was engaged. His uneasiness mounted, but now it was too late to turn back. There was every chance that he might be traveling the road to perdition, Peter thought gloomily—except that the road over which Peter and his comrades rode actually led to Yorktown, a peaceful and godfearing little village.

November's chilly winds blew gustily. Already the song birds had begun winging southward, except for the cardinal and the mockingbird. Frosty sunlight peeped through the trees, transformed the tall grass in the marshes into a golden carpet, and cast sparkling glints over the river. Geese honked overhead. The tracks of a fox crossed the road.

A comrade rode up beside Peter and spoke in an easy, matter-of-fact manner. "First, we must be sure the tea is on board the ship," he said.

"Do you mean we've come all this way on a mere rumor?"

The other laughed. "'Tis no rumor. We've good evidence there are two half-chests of tea aboard, assigned to Prentis & Company of Williamsburg."

Peter's eyes half closed as he visualized the small brick storehouse on Duke of Gloucester Street where Prentis &

Company was located. He had never looked upon William Prentis as a special villain, and he wondered if too much ale had clouded his head and led him to agree to this expedition.

Filled with misgivings, he asked:"So we reach Yorktown harbor, board the ship, find the tea, and then what?"

"We wait for word from Williamsburg as to what to do next," the comrade answered.

"And if the word never comes?"

"Then I guess we act as our best judgment tells us!"

Afterward Peter confessed the whole affair to Anne. He didn't make light of the discomfiture he had felt on the ride from Williamsburg to Yorktown, or conceal his conviction that serious trouble might develop from subsequent events.

"We reached Yorktown," Peter told Anne, "and rode down the narrow street to the wharves, and found the ship *Virginia* riding peacefully in the harbor. We boarded her, and the captain, a rather decent fellow, admitted he had the tea."

Peter fidgeted, telling the story. "You've come to get it?" the captain asked.

"Aye,"one of the Williamsburg party replied.

"You've a paper from Prentis & Company?"

"We need no paper for this business," the Williamsburg buck said breezily.

A grab was made for the two chests. Up went the first, in a single mighty heave, then over the rail it sailed and into the water with a loud, ugly splash.

Peter said the scuffle that followed then should have been expected.

"Those sailors had a spirit too," he assured Anne. "We finally got that second chest to the rail, but not before I received this nasty crack on the head. A watery-eyed fellow came at me with a club. Luckily the blow glanced off. He might have cracked my skull wide open."

A lump the size of a goose egg gave Peter's head a lop-sided appearance. "What happened next?" Anne asked.

"Then we rode home," Peter said simply. "We had taken the law in our hands own and staged our own Boston Tea Party. I can't say I think it a very proud business."

"And the others?"

"There are those who feel chesty. It was a lark in the name of patriotism or liberty or whatever you'd call it. And there won't be any of the tea drunk in Williamsburg—of that we can be sure."

Anne sighed. She supposed Peter wanted to be reassured that no trouble would follow, and that in a way he had acted for a good principle (which, honestly, she believed), and she said:"I've heard of a tempest in a teapot. I guess you could call it that and put it out of your mind."

Peter nodded. Some day, he thought, if an honest man engraved his tombstone, a slab in the graveyard beside Bruton Church would read:

Here lies
PETER SMITH
Reluctant Patriot

He glanced at Anne and smiled sheepishly.

George Wythe had other worries. For twenty years now he had lived in his brick mansion on the Palace Green, and during that time he had seen many governors of Virginia drive past his gate. Fauquier had been Wythe's favorite, an intimate friend. Lord Botetourt at heart had been a man of strong character, stout principles, and kindly spirit. Lord Dunmore, who presently occupied the Palace, presented another problem.

Fireworks had lighted the skies over Williamsburg on the night when Lord Dunmore had arrived to become the new Governor and the *Virginia Gazette* had acknowledged the capital's "Gratitude to his Majesty for appointing a Nobleman of his Abilities and good Character to preside over us." But in the span between 1771 and 1774 a feeling of uneasy change developed. Lord Dunmore's popularity couldn't equal that of Fauquier or Lord Botetourt. To say that he was more arrogant than they had been wasn't quite correct, for the word suggested a strutting peacock, and there was more to the failing of Lord Dunmore than this. Testiness, ill humor, suspicion, quick temper, intemperate impulse—in various ways, each of these terms might apply. That was the trouble, actually. Lord Dunmore had a tendency of giving those who dealt with him an impression of walking on eggshells.

Yet outwardly, as early December of 1774 approached, friendly glances were cast by the townspeople when they strolled by the Palace. As a friend told Obediah Holiday, the wig-maker, "The women folk talk a lot about the new baby Lady Dunmore is expecting. I guess it's an experience we can understand. We've all been babies."

Obediah nodded, conceding the point with some effort. His friend was a stout man, a human barrel who wore the clothes around his middle in rolls resembling a barrel's hoops. At some time in life he must have been smaller.

Before the first week of December ended, the Palace heard the lusty squalls of a new daughter. "The young Virginian is in perfect health,"reported the *Virginia Gazette*, echoing the general feeling of good will in the capital.

The new year began. People said,"It's 1775,"a figure that seemed to have a nice crisp, rounded sound. Three-quarters way through the eighteenth century...it was a year to make older folk smile and forget a few birthdays and say, "We'll be here when the new century rolls around. We'll live to see the year 1800." And how much all their lives would change —not in ten years or twenty-five years, but within months— didn't bother anyone greatly. Who can foresee the future?

In mid-January Lady Dunmore's daughter was baptized Virginia, in honor of the colony. The Palace glistened with candlelight, and Williamsburg wondered if there ever had been a more elegant ball in all its long years. Again, fireworks lighted the sky. A baby stood for hope, a brightening future. The omen for the new year was fine.

In March Peter journeyed to Richmond upon business that gave him considerably more satisfaction than his jaunt to Yorktown the previous November. Now that Peter had completed his apprenticeship, he continued at the shop as a journeyman silversmith, and his responsibilities were far broader. A chance to secure some old silver plate that could be melted down and used again brought Peter to Richmond. Terms satisfactory to both parties were arranged and Peter, in high spirits, announced that he would leave immediately for the return trip to Williamsburg.

A frown creased the brow of the Richmond merchant.

"You mean you are not even going to look in on the great debate at St. John's Church?"

Peter felt embarrassed. Truly, the merchant must think him a dunderhead for having forgotten this meeting, but he had been so concerned with his own affairs that all other events had been pushed into the back of his mind. Now he said, rather lamely, "Why, yes—of course I will!"

"After all," the merchant said, "this second Virginia convention would be meeting in Williamsburg at this very moment if it had not been for the appearance of that British man-of-war. What else was there to do but come to Richmond with that threat of armed intervention waiting right at your back door?"

"There was no other choice," Peter agreed.

"But where will this unrest end, my dear young fellow?"

"It is something it doesn't do too much good to think about," Peter confessed, supposing that he was still the reluctant patriot.

Later that afternoon he made his way to St. John's Church, seeing first the big white steeple topped by a cross. He opened the gate and walked through the old graveyard, sauntering slowly and sensing at once a suppressed excitement in the crowd milling around the door. Peter needed only ears to understand the point of the great debate among the delegates:

"Patrick Henry is right! Virginia should assemble and train its own militia! I'd say he had made the right motion."

"The conservatives are against him."

"Jefferson isn't, from what I hear."

"If that motion carries, it will be because Henry refuses to be talked down!"

Peter pushed his way to where he could watch the delegates. He listened, as ten years ago short of a few weeks Jefferson had first eavesdropped on the back-country Patrick in the debate on the Stamp Act. Bewigged now, but as sharp-nosed as ever, with those long fingers still opening and closing and exerting a kind of magic over his audience, the Son of Thunder had lost none of his power. How like a stream in spring, swollen by rains and sweeping all obstacles before it, did that voice still flow on. Peter stood silent, moved, won completely by this man who cried:

"Is life so dear, or peace so sweet, as to be purchased at the price of chains and slavery? Forbid it, Almighty God! I know not what course others may take, but as for me, give me liberty or give me death!"

On the hard ride home to Williamsburg, Peter never for a moment doubted why, in the end, the motion to assemble and arm the Virginia militia had carried. Had he been a delegate, the passionate fervor of Patrick Henry would have captured him. He, too, would have leaped to his feet, shouting "Aye! Aye!"

Yet back in Williamsburg, Peter tried to put from his mind thoughts of the threatening British man-of-war or the arming of the militia. He was a man with work to do. And he watched the crocuses opening and dreamed still of the shop he would one day own, the house he would one day build.

At the print shop young Johnny Jarratt also was a lad with work to do those days. Early April brought the first truly warm weather to the Virginia Peninsula. On days when there was a job to put through the press, hours were often long. So that April twentieth when Johnny at last finished he had, as he said, pulled the devil's tail until his howls could be heard all over the lower regions.

Darkness had settled over Duke of Gloucester Street for many hours when Johnny washed off the last ink-ball, snuffed out the last candle, and locked the door. He stretched wearily and thought that tonight he could sleep standing in the stocks before the Public Gaol. Around him Williamsburg seemed deeply quiet—an old town that had donned its nightcap and tucked itself into bed—and then Johnny heard, or thought he heard, muffled sounds. Of voices. Of horses neighing.

The direction of the disturbance—why that word popped into his mind, he was never sure afterward—seemed to be Market Square. Wide awake now, Johnny set off to investigate. Then he saw the lanterns at the Powder Magazine, the horses hitched to the covered wagon, the men in the garb of British marines.

These marines could only come from one place—that British sloop *Magdalen*, on station off the lower Peninsula. And if the marines were here, Governor Dunmore had to send for them. Why? Because he was alarmed at the arming of the militia? And was having the guns and powder moved from the Magazine before local troops could seize it?

Johnny had guessed accurately. Lord Dunmore would admit that he feared what the militia might do. And whether Johnny or someone else gave the warning of the Governor's plot, the subsequent events, as Lord Dunmore himself described them, found the town of Williamsburg ripping off its nightcap and leaping from its bed.

Rat-a-tat-tat! Drums beat furiously—down Duke of Glou-

cester Street, Nicholson, Francis, across Market Square, the
Palace Green.

Running footfalls—the curse of a man tripping over a dog
in the darkness—the sound of a musket slapping against a
jacket—and hoarse voices, shouting:

"Drummer, why are you pounding like a crazy drunkard?"

"The powder! Dunmore's stealing the powder!"

"Get your gun! Come! the British marines are taking our
gunpowder!"

Swiftly, Williamsburg's militia tumbled into the streets,
guns in hand, forming into the best order they could. People
appeared everywhere—from the houses, the taverns. Older
children shouted and one little girl began to cry. The dogs
barked furiously. Over all this din still other voices rasped
shrilly:

"To the Palace!"

"We'll hang the Governor for this!"

The British marines had made their getaway—the powder was gone—and tempers flared higher.

Inside the Palace, Governor Dunmore paced hallways that only three months before had glistened with the lights of the elegant ball in honor of his daughter's christening. Now Lady Dunmore could tell that he feared for their safety.

"All the people assembled," Lord Dunmore wrote afterward, still seeming to be shaken by the memory, "and during their consultation, continual threats were brought to my house, that it was their resolution to seize upon, or massacre me, and every person found giving me assistance if I refused to deliver the powder immediately into their custody."

But the powder, bouncing in the wagon over dark roads,

was no longer within the Governor's reach. Soon it would be securely aboard the *Fowey*, where Lord Dunmore wished he and his family were also.

Midnight passed. The crowd surged over the Palace Green, pushed against the gate, shouted, hooted. Clammy hands grasped musket stocks. Threats, ridicule, scornful cries still rang through the night.

"Hang the Governor!"

"Give us back the powder and we'll blow up the Palace!"

"His Lordship's moving from room to room—looking for a bigger bed to hide under!"

Some carried torches and lanterns. The quivering lights revealed taut faces, and eyes that were growing wearier. A few drifted away, then others and still others. Presently a quiet settled back over the town, but now it was an ominous silence, for many people were angry to the marrow of their bones and neither Lord Dunmore nor Williamsburg had heard the last of this episode.

Father broke off his story to ask Jane, "This happened during the night and early morning of April 20 and 21. Do you see how it fitted a kind of pattern in history?"

Jane hesitated, looking puzzled. But Father's formula for a poor batter at history must have been working, for I had been reading the night before about the old Powder Magazine on Market Square and I said: "It was April 19 that, at Lexington and Concord, the embattled Massachusetts farmers fired the shot heard round the world."

Jane, who is a wizard for memorizing poetry, recited from Longfellow:

How the farmers gave them ball for ball,
From behind each fence and farmyard wall,
Chasing the redcoats down the lane,
Then crossing the fields to emerge again
Under the trees at the turn of the road,
And only pausing to fire and load.

So, too, was Patrick Henry ready to chase the redcoats when at Hanover Courthouse he heard of the battles of Lexington and Concord and the seizure of the gunpowder at Williamsburg. Patrick mustered the militia and marched down the Peninsula with blood in his eye. The *Virginia Gazette* said boldly: "The Sword is now drawn, and God knows when it will be sheathed."

With about one hundred and fifty armed men, gathered along the route of march, Patrick Henry appeared near Williamsburg on May third. He demanded that the colony be paid for the powder the Governor had ordered seized, and angry citizens backed up the demand by standing guard over the public treasury. Hard words passed between the Governor and the people, the Assembly, and Patrick's militia. Finally the Governor capitulated and the Receiver-General gave the colony a draft for 330 pounds—about twice what the powder was worth!

"And for the remainder of the story," Jane said," I give you Thomas Jefferson and George Washington!"

Father shook his head. "You're forgetting a very important person," he insisted. "I mean the other George—George Mason."

CHAPTER TEN

The Other George

FOR ALMOST AS LONG as there had been English-men in Virginia, George Masons had lived there. In 1620, when the colony was little more than a troubled strip between the deep sea and the wilderness controlled by the Indians, the first George Mason had reached America. Sometime in the early 1650's this hardy adventurer traveled up the Potomac and staked out a claim to a plantation on the rich lowlands of the Northern Neck. Other George Masons had followed until in 1725 the fourth George Mason was born.

When the lad was ten his father died, but his mother possessed spunk and perseverance and a will of her own, and her son had a happy boyhood. When in later years George Mason number four closed his eyes and thought back over his youth, what did he remember?

For one thing he recalled the tiny piece of paper—no bigger than a coin the size of a shilling—on which every word of the Lord's Prayer was clearly written. For another, there was his mother's brooch, studded with garnets resembling nail heads for the brooch was shaped like a Golden Horseshoe. This piece of jewelry had been a gift to George's father from Governor Spotswood, and it commemorated an historic episode.

Doubtless the third George Mason recounted to the fourth George Mason the adventures he had encountered as a member of an expedition of fifty men who had been the first to explore across the Blue Ridge Mountains. But the Knightly Order of the Golden Horseshoe, organized by the Governor after the journey across the Blue Ridge, drew its most attractive tradition from Spotswood's appearance in Albany in 1722 to sign a treaty with the Indians of the Six Nations. To the speaker for the tribes the Governor also presented a Golden Horseshoe.

"Whenever any of your men come as an emissary to Virginia," Governor Spotswood said, "have him bring this horseshoe as a token and he will be recognized at once as a friend of our people."

So the younger George, gazing at his mother's brooch, always hoped that one day an Indian would come wearing the Governor's token. In a way, that dream did come true, for one day an Indian was brought to the Mason house, the son of a Susquehannock chief who had been injured on a raid.

The poor Indian lad was in bad condition. For several days young George watched him, wondering if he could go on struggling for his breath in such a desperate manner. When George tried to feed the boy with a spoon, the jaws were locked so tightly that the food could not be forced between his teeth. The Masons gave up hope for the Indian's recovery, but a friend said that the lad might be a victim of evil spirits, in which case baptism might save him. So George watched the sick boy baptized—and soon the closed eyes opened, the locked jaws relaxed.

"It was true," said the son of the Susquehannock chief when he had recovered. "I had been pawewawd." That word in English meant "bewitched."

George may have believed this story, or if he didn't he had a native politeness that led him to hold his tongue. His quick mind absorbed learning easily, and by the time he came of age he was marked as a leader. He built a fine new home on the shores of the Potomac, took his place on the governing bodies in the town of Alexandria, the court of Fairfax County and the vestry of his parish church, and managed his plantation with wisdom and care.

One saw George Mason on the streets of Alexandria as a resplendent figure. A coat of brown velvet covered a yellow waistcoat. At neck and wrists lace ruffles showed. Good dark eyes and a prominent forehead were emphasized by a dark wig. In every way he looked like a man who led a prosperous, contented life, and who wanted the world to remain precisely as it was. Yet one day when he gave his oldest son a plantation, the mark of the fourth George's mind and sentiments was in the name he bestowed upon the place. He called it "Lexington," after the famous battle.

George Mason had a large family—nine children in all—and to prove he didn't play favorites, when he built his new home there was a window apiece to light the beds for the young Masons who between 1753 and 1770 came along on schedule like well-run stagecoaches. It is doubtful if on the Northern Neck George Mason had a closer friend than Washington. The two Georges were seen frequently together—at private functions, in public at meetings concerned with the governmental affairs of their district. When in 1759 Washington went to Williamsburg as a new member of the House of Burgesses, Mason went with him.

One term in the Assembly at Williamsburg was enough for George Mason. The long debates irritated him, the committee meetings made him suffer at the thought of all the time they wasted, and he preferred remaining in the background and helping Washington win reelection year after year. Ill health may have led him also to withdraw from public life.

In many situations, however, Washington called on Mason for advice and even to draft resolutions, as in the case of the agreements reached at that first meeting of the dissolved Bur-

gesses in Raleigh Tavern. Sitting in bed, weakened by a convulsive colic that let him sip little more than a weak milk punch, George Mason gladly put his thoughts on paper for his friend.

Thoughts and thoughts and thoughts...George Mason's mind churned them around constantly, as a gristmill grinds flour. No man in Virginia had more ideas about the functions and obligations of government. Then came the crisis in the spring of 1775, and in that emergency Virginia called upon the source of enormous strength that quiet, modest, retiring George Mason had become.

Meanwhile in Williamsburg Patrick Henry was feeling fine over the way he had handled the gunpowder episode. With the Governor's bond for 330 pounds in pocket, Patrick withdrew the militia, writing a fellow member of the House of Burgesses that "the affair of the powder is now settled so as to produce satisfaction to me, and I earnestly wish to the Colony in general."

Unhappily the incident wouldn't stay settled. On the first of June Lord Dunmore opened a tense session of the Assembly. George Mason had come to Williamsburg, as eager as anyone to hear the report of Peyton Randolph, who had recently returned from presiding over the First Continental Congress.

Something was in the air—a sense of unrest, principally— that Mason's keen mind grasped at once. As he wrote a friend in London on the day before the Williamsburg meeting began, Americans were welded together by "the blood lately shed at Boston." Mason did not doubt what this spirit would mean to the colonists: "There are no difficulties or hardships which they are not determined to encounter with firmness and perseverance."

The unrest in Williamsburg also was sensed by Johnny Jarratt. He heard about the scheme of some of the young bloods in town. Maybe he was one of the youths who on the night of June second descended on the Powder Magazine. What these youngsters expected to do after they "captured" the arsenal even they couldn't have said exactly.

Hearts beat with a thump-thump-thump as feet crept stealthily across the grass of Market Square. In the darkness the eight-sided Magazine loomed like the shadow of some bulky, misshapen monster. A hoarse voice whispered:

"Try the main entrance."

Excited, quivering hands reached the portal, pushed.

Along Duke of Gloucester Street heads lifted at the sound of the detonation. A flash and then a roar, some cried, trying to describe what they had just seen and heard. Men started running for Market Square.

Several of the young raiders were injured, some badly. Investigation soon revealed what had happened. Dunmore had ordered a spring gun trained on the entrance to the arsenal. He had, in effect, prepared for war with his own townspeople.

On June eighth Lord Dunmore fled with his family to a British warship. No one wept to see him go.

Events now moved at a dizzy pace. On June 24 the Burgesses adjourned, nine days after the Second Continental Congress appointed George Washington commander-in-chief of combined colonial forces. The war had come in earnest, and at least one citizen known to all who passed down Duke of Gloucester Street posted a notice that demonstrated he had no intention of standing idly by:

> *To all Gentlemen and Others who have patronized me in the Past, I beg leave to say that I have gone off to fight under the glorious Banner of the Continental Union, for Home and Country and against Tyranny.*
>
> *Obediah Holiday. Late Wig Maker,*
> *now Sergeant Major,*
> *Williamsburg Militia*

Peter showed Anne the notice and grinned. Yes, he too— the reluctant patriot—felt the same as Obediah Holiday. He handled a musket gingerly as though it were a hot ingot of silver.

"You couldn't hit a rabbit," Anne said crossly.

"I'll learn."

The whole town had gone a bit daft, Anne decided. Patrick Henry was back in Williamsburg, now the grim-faced commander-in-chief of all the Virginia forces gathering at the capital. Drums rolled, soldiers-to-be like Peter paraded and drilled as they wore the grass bare on Market Square. In autumn aboard the British man-of-war Lord Dunmore declared that Virginia was under martial law, and in succeeding months he directed attacks by sea against the coastal counties. When in January, 1776, Norfolk was burned, Williamsburg learned of another example of Lord Dunmore's hostility.

"We were well rid of that bird," Johnny Jarratt said, expressing the general sentiment.

After Lord Dunmore fled to safety aboard a British man-of-war, the House of Burgesses tried three times to carry on its work. Somehow enough members never assembled. On May 6, 1776, the Burgesses declared their work finished, ending 157 years as the oldest representative body of government in British America. Through most of those years the Burgesses had fought for one principle with a square-jawed resolution. Virginians had the sole right to tax Virginians!

Yet on the day the House of Burgesses ceased to exist, Williamsburg seemed only to be casting off an old love to embrace a new. The taverns and coffee houses were as busy as ever. Carriages, coaches, horsemen churned up the dust along Duke of Gloucester Street. From the Tidewater, from the western farm lands, from over the mountains delegates assembled for a new Virginia Convention. And they spoke now a word of bold defiance, the word "independence."

"I'll tell you what the instructions of my people are," announced the delegate from Cumberland County. "As for any allegiance to his Britannic Majesty, I'm to bid him a good night forever!"

On the fifteenth of May the Convention listened to resolutions directing the Virginia delegates at the Continental Congress to move that the United Colonies were free and independent states. Yes, sir, said the delegate from Cumberland County, those were his sentiments. Nor was he alone— the resolutions were carried by an unanimous vote.

Johnny Jarratt heard the news and flung his cap into the air. In Waller's Grove next day most of the citizens of Williamsburg gathered to hear the resolutions read to the army. Then three toasts were given—the first to the American independent states. Soldiers fired artillery and small arms. The people cheered.

"Now," cried the spokesman, "a toast to the Grand Congress of the United States and their respective legislatures."

Again the guns roared, the citizens yelled.

"And a toast, ladies and gentlemen, to General Washington —and victory to the American arms!"

Once more the guns flashed, the cheers thundered. Above the Capitol spanked the new Grand Union Flag of the American states. Spirits soared higher, then even higher. The soldiers were a trim lot, parading smartly, handling those muskets like veterans. And that new national banner, catching the wind and rippling with a proud defiance from its staff, made hearts thump, breaths quicken, eyes grow misty. That night fireworks dazzled the celebrants who tumbled out of houses and taverns to watch the displays. The spirit of everyone's feelings was captured the following day in nine words that appeared in the masthead of the *Virginia Gazette*:

THIRTEEN UNITED COLONIES
"United, we stand—Divided, we fall."

On Friday, May 17, Bruton Church opened its doors for a day of fasting and prayer. That afternoon George Mason returned to Williamsburg, a quiet little man who in his own quiet way now stepped forward to take his place as the principal actor upon the stage of history.

George Mason's tired eyes, his strained face disclosed the "smart fit of the gout" that had kept him from the earlier session of the Convention. Declaring independence was one thing—what did it mean until a plan of government was worked out? Walking along Duke of Gloucester Street, bumping elbows with the delegates from the far-flung counties that composed Virginia—delegates who ranged from the plantation owners of the Tidewater to the wild Irish who had settled beyond the Blue Ridge and couldn't stand strangers near them—Mason must have wondered how all their heads ever could be knocked together so that they would agree to any plan.

Mason saw them all, drinking at the Raleigh Tavern, eating with forks and sometimes with fingers in the taverns, talking loudly and resting on their squirrel guns as they sniffed at the dandies in their velvets and satins. He saw the frontiersmen who liked to make up laws as they needed them, and the Germans and Scotch and Pennsylvania Dutch who were standoffish and suspicious. Across Market Square coon-

skin cap mingled with curled wig and Mason must have
thought that there was Virginia's big problem in a single
glance—to plan a government that would fit under both!

In the room Mason occupied he read the resolutions declaring Virginia's independence. The preamble was worse
than long and tedious—it was almost timid. Appointed to
the committee that was to draw up a plan of government, his
irritation was ill disguised. All committees wasted time, and
this one, he told a friend, was "overcharged with useless
members." Cynically he added:

"We shall, in all probability, have a thousand ridiculous
and impracticable proposals, and of course a plan formed of
heterogeneous, jarring and unintelligible ingredients."

Underneath all this crustiness, Mason set his jaw. Probably
two or three men would have to roll up their sleeves, keep
their wits, and do this job. In large measure, Mason alone did
it. His quill pen scratched in a firm, round script—writing
words about government that frontiersman and planter,
farmer and merchant, tight-lipped Dutchman and wild-eyed
Irishman from across the Blue Ridge must accept first if they
would govern wisely:

"...all Men are by Nature equally free and independent,
and have certain inherent Rights, of which, when they enter
into a State of Society, they cannot, by any Compact, de-
prive or divest their Posterity; namely, the Enjoyment of
Life and Liberty, with the Means of acquiring and possessing
Property, and pursuing and obtaining Happiness and Safety."

From where did a people derive the power to govern
themselves? That power, Mason wrote, came from God and
Nature. Therefore, a government was organized for the "com-

mon benefit, protection, and security of the people, nation, or community." No man, no set of men, deserved special privileges. No officer, no judge should gain power through mere heredity. Powers of government should be kept separated, so that one group made the laws, another administered them, and a third judged their fairness.

Mason's mind grasped the image of a land that protected both the man in the curled wig and the coonskin cap. Elections should be held freely, honestly, openly. No law ever should be suspended without the consent of the representatives of the people. In rights of property, as well as in suits between man and man, the ancient custom of trial by jury should be "held sacred."

Freedom was a word that George Mason understood, and as his pen scratched on freedom became a responsibility to define and to transform into a way of life. Thus he recognized freedom of the press as "one of the great bulwarks of liberty" and only a despotic government ever would wish to destroy it. In times of emergency armies were needed, but in times of peace standing armies probably were "dangerous to liberty" and in all cases the elected representatives of the people and not the generals or admirals should hold supreme authority.

Yet had he said enough? This document, which he entitled Declaration of Rights, must serve Virginia, but as the first such document to be written in America, it must apply also to the will and the spirit of what the *Virginia Gazette* had called the thirteen United Colonies. Freedom was a "blessing" that had to be deserved. Mason's mind sought precise words to make the people understand how they must act if they would be free. They must be just—firmly just. They must be moderate and temperate. They must respect frugality and virtue. They must act always according to fundamental principles.

Even in religion—"the duty we owe our Creator"—they must act "only by reason and conviction, not by force or violence." All men should worship according to conscience, knowing that "it is the mutual duty of all to practise Christian forbearance, love, and charity towards each other."

Virginia's Declaration of Rights went before the Convention. For two weeks George Mason heard his ideas debated, but only a few slight changes and additions were suggested. Then the delegates from the tidewater and the valley of the Shenandoah and from over the Blue Ridge stood up to vote. They all understood in a way what George Mason had given them—a basic blueprint of what a workable American democracy must be.

"Aye," voted the man from the tidewater.

"Aye," voted the western farmer.

"Aye," voted the frontiersman from the mountains.

George Mason tramped back to his room, glad that he could soon return home.

Jane sighed. "He was a wonderful, wise old fellow—for all his bark and growl."

"Perhaps I exaggerated that," Father said.

Anyhow, couriers carried to the Continental Congress Virginia's resolutions for independence and its Declaration of Rights. In Philadelphia one of Williamsburg's best loved men labored on another document, so similar in many ideas—the Declaration of Independence.

Meanwhile, under its own new constitution, the Conven-

tion in Williamsburg moved to elect a governor. The choice
was made on the first ballot.

"Patrick Henry," I said.

Father laughed. Really, you had to remember that day
when Patrick rode down Duke of Gloucester Street on his
lean sorrel horse, greased pigtail flapping, homespun knee-
breeches wrapped round the saddle, to understand how he
had changed. For on the day of the inaugural at the Palace,
up stepped Patrick Henry—handsome in a fine black suit,
resplendent in a scarlet cloak, a symbol of prim dignity in a
powdered wig.

But troubled days were ahead for Williamsburg. In 1779
Thomas Jefferson followed Henry as governor, and fear that
the enemy might invade the Peninsula led to moving the
capital to Richmond.

The year 1781 brought the bitterest trials. The traitor,
Benedict Arnold, marched a British force into eastern Virginia. Then from the south another British force appeared
under Cornwallis. A plucky American force under the Marquis de Lafayette joined with small bands of militia to outwit
a combined British force of about seven thousand, not giving
the redcoats the battle they wanted and felt they could easily
win, but rather nipping at them like a terrier that is an infernal
nuisance but too lively to be caught and spanked.

Through hot June Lord Cornwallis marched down the
Peninsula, wary of the Americans who followed at his heels
(but at a safe distance) and in far from the best of spirits. It was
certainly an ill day for Williamsburg when he marched into
town.

CHAPTER ELEVEN

The World Turned Upside Down

LORD CORNWALLIS knew how to nourish a hot temper. He brooded over a peeve, a slight, a bad turn in luck. His anger always seemed to simmer and then boil. Then, when his big nose began to twitch, his deep eyes to crackle, his full mouth to tighten, his double chin to quiver, the explosion was not unlike steam rushing out of a boiler. Some contemporaries describe his face as turning purple with rage—and a flashy spectacle that must have made against his red coat, his glittering buttons, the sash that held his sword-case.

Unhappily for Williamsburg, his lordship's mood had been strained almost to the breaking point when the British troops swarmed down Duke of Gloucester Street. Cornwallis took over the house of the president of William and Mary and left that poor man to sleep wherever he could—in a haystack, for all Cornwallis cared.

Ten days of terror followed. Redcoats overran taverns, homes, seizing any food they could find. Citizens unable to escape in advance of the British forces soon faced famine. Slaves were confiscated. As though human conquest were not bitter enough to withstand, a dense swarm of flies settled upon Williamsburg. Smallpox became rampant.

Weak from want of food, sick at heart, girls like Anne avoided going outdoors whenever they could. Dreams at night easily could grow jumbled, frightening, filled with evil portents that lingered through the next day. Then night again and more dreams. . . .

So gloom of day mingled with the despair of night. Memories now lost their meaning—events of only a few years ago seemed to belong to another century, another world. Vaguely one remembered the old Williamsburg, swarming with its Burgesses who had tramped up to Raleigh Tavern in defiance of the Governor, the bells ringing and the guns firing on the day Virginia had declared her independence, the solemn hours of prayer and fasting in Bruton Church, the jaunty

faces of the men who had changed history—Washington and Wythe and Jefferson, Peyton Randolph and Patrick Henry and George Mason, Obediah Holiday, the boys who had been injured storming the Powder Magazine...one remembered, wondering what it all had meant with Cornwallis and his redcoats crushing the town beneath their heels.

Brave words, proud acts, a new flag fluttering over the Capitol—and now, not liberty, not independence, but conquest, hunger, smallpox, insult and outrage!

For Anne, what dreams? Of Peter somewhere with the forces under Lafayette—of Peter who one night seemed to appear so full of life and defiance and whose face the next night dimmed and drifted away into nothingness as though he were already dead?

Then Williamsburg heard from boastful redcoats news that seemed to crush hope, to break the last wavering spirits. Somewhere near Jamestown, Lafayette had met the British in a large skirmish or small battle—such details always were exaggerated or guessed at. By British accounts the Americans had been sharply defeated, had fallen across the river, and were beating a hot retreat to their base at Portsmouth.

Yet the reports must have been true since on July fourth Cornwallis and his troops moved from Williamsburg. The old town shook itself like a whipped person who ached all over.

That summer General George Washington watched the British in New York from a base on the upper Hudson River. Couriers brought him information of Cornwallis and the British down on the Virginia Peninsula. Washington's dark eyes brightened. If combined American forces were thrown against Cornwallis there, he was trapped unless he could receive reinforcements or escape by sea! After six weary years of war, Washington saw at last his chance—to win!

Along the upper Hudson the roads echoed with the sounds of an army on the move. Off the capes of Chesapeake Bay, twenty-four French warships under Admiral Comte de Grasse dropped anchor—grim watchdogs determined that there would be no escape, no reinforcements. Meanwhile Cornwallis, who could avoid battle in this trap simply by crossing the river, making all of Carolina his future battlefield, waited as though dazed by a hypnotic spell.

September brought the sound of other marching feet along the road to Williamsburg. General Washington was returning to his "Metropolis."

At about four o'clock in the afternoon the cry raced up Duke of Gloucester Street:

"Washington's coming!"

Colonel St. George Tucker, who lived in Williamsburg and served as an officer in the Virginia Militia, watched the General's arrival, and memories of that wonderful moment filled the letter he wrote his wife:

"He approached without any pomp or parade, attended only by a few horsemen and his own servants. The Count de Rochambeau and General Hand, with one or two more officers were with him. . . . To my great surprise he recognized my features and spoke to me immediately by name."

Then the Marquis de Lafayette rode up on his horse, and Colonel Tucker said:

"Never was more joy painted in any countenance than

theirs. The Marquis rode up with precipitation, clasped the
General in his arms and embraced him with an ardor not
easily described."

Men, women, children, soldiers, dogs—as Colonel Tucker
declared, the whole town seemed in motion. Brigade by
brigade, as Washington reviewed the troops, the artillery
fired its salute. The townspeople, Tucker wrote, "seemed to
vie with each other in demonstrations of joy and eagerness
to see their beloved countryman."

How much did Washington remember, coming back to Williamsburg after six grim years? Did he recall the boy who had ridden down Duke of Gloucester street in quest of his surveyor's license? Or the young man four years later who had made the great trek into the Ohio wilderness? Or the soldier who liked to finish whatever he started planting the British flag in the embers of Fort Duquesne? Or the ring he had bought for Patsy Custis, the fine balls at the Palace where he had danced with his wife, the plays that had enchanted him night after night, the Apollo Room at the Raleigh that had been a Rebel's Roost for Burgesses who would bleed and die before they would surrender the basic principles of self-government?

Washington's headquarters were at the home of George Wythe on Palace Green—and what memories might that old place reveal, if houses could only talk! Down this green expanse had walked young men, still untested, the world before them—Jefferson, Patrick Henry, Washington himself. By this door had ridden royal governors, and one had fled to escape the wrath of the people. So had history, flowing like a stream, eddied and turned here—changing its course, cutting a gorge that deepened and widened. And the stream had grown into a rapids, a cascade. It had broken away old barriers and found new horizons called freedom and liberty and independence!

Williamsburg during the next few days learned to adjust to new faces, new personalities. At the King's Arms Tavern lived that sharp-tongued soldier of fortune who styled himself Baron von Steuben. This fierce old Prussian, swearing in three languages, was the drillmaster who had tongue-lashed

ragged farm boys into seasoned, well-disciplined soldiers—
teaching them how to handle a musket, that bayonets were
not intended to be used for icepicks, screaming "Ja! Ja! Like
dot, you dunderhead! Hold it so—Ja! Ja!" Von Steuben's
methods had worked and he served now as Inspector General
of Washington's army. Von Steuben did all things extrava-
gantly—his bill at King's Arms Tavern for lodging, ale and
the keep of his servants ran to almost $300.

The distinguished commander of the French expedition-
ary forces, Comte de Rochambeau, made his headquarters in
Peyton Randolph's house on Market Square, and Mrs. Randolph—Williamsburg knew her as "Aunt Betty"— pronounced him a thorough gentleman.

So Williamsburg watched the four great men—Washington and Lafayette, von Steuben and de Rochambeau—walking its streets, meeting, talking, planning, waiting. Washington's troops, Colonel Tucker wrote his wife, were coming
down the bay, adding:

"Cornwallis may now tremble for his fate, for nothing but
some extraordinary interposition of his guardian angels seems
capable of saving him and the whole army from captivity."

The day was September 28, the sun had not yet risen.
Through the darkness rose the beat of drums. Lights flickered
in the sleeping city. Heads peeped from doors, dogs barked,
forms moved noiselessly along the road. Voices spoke through
the early morning mists.

"What is it?"

"Washington's troops are marching on."

"After Cornwallis?"

"To pay him back for what he did to us!"

The sun came up, disclosing the dust from columns of marching feet, stomping horses, the wheels of supply wagons, the rolling guns.

Then Williamsburg could only pray and wait.

Distantly, Williamsburg heard the rumble of guns at Yorktown. Cornwallis was caught, neatly, hopelessly, his defenses pounded by French guns while Americans cheered and by American guns while Frenchmen cheered. On the morning of October 17 all of the guns under Washington's command seemed to be pounding in unison. Forenoon saw an officer approaching under a flag of truce. Surrender—it must mean surrender!

The negotiations between Washington and Cornwallis consumed another day. At dawn the Americans listened to bagpipes playing across the British lines. Along the beach at Yorktown many persons seemed to be moving, and out in the harbor glimpses could be caught of the top gallant masts of great vessels. At two o'clock the final agreement of capitulation was received.

Three weeks after leaving Williamsburg—on October 19, 1781—Washington mounted his elegant horse. In two trim colums, Americans on one side and French on the other, his troops waited for the British to march through and ground their arms in final surrender. Lord Cornwallis, pleading illness, did not appear, but he issued new uniforms to his men— a last proud defiance against the dark hour. A British band struck up the sad tune, "The World Turned Upside Down."

The news raced up the rivers and over the mountains. Williamsburg celebrated as Philadelphia celebrated and Boston celebrated.

And in Williamsburg, as in many towns across the colonies, girls like Anne walked alone to the road down which the returning troops would come—wondering if he would look older and different and wiser, if he would walk straight or perhaps limp, if his gun would seem heavy on his shoulder, and what he'd say and what she'd say too....

But the breezes, creeping over the bay and river, winging with the geese and ducks across the golden marshes, ruffling the tall grass in the fields and swirling the dust along the road, sang a song that she heard in her heart.

The country was free and at peace and the years ahead were rich with hope and opportunity.

So the war ended, not at Yorktown, nor at the peace table in Paris, but silently and sweetly in all those hearts where victory meant home and family, work and faith.

CHAPTER TWELVE

The Ghost and the Genie

OLD WILLIAMSBURG suffered hard years after the Revolution. With the capital now at Richmond, tradesmen moved away, and the population dwindled. Empty buildings seemed to lose their spirit, their wish to survive. Some crumbled into ruins, fire destroyed others. A battle fought here between Union and Confederate forces during the War Between the States added to the destruction and decay.

Once the old town shook itself, and appeared to come to life, when in 1824 the gallant Lafayette revisited Williamsburg. Again there was a gay spirit along Duke of Gloucester Street, a banquet at Raleigh Tavern. But the hour of brightness was brief. A traveler to Williamsburg three years later recorded sadly, "I thought I was transported to Noah's Ark, when I first came into this town, so prodigious was the quantity of animals I met with, without seeing a single person till I reached the post office."

In a way, the ghost wouldn't have minded that, for dogs always had liked him, anyhow. Yet one wing of the Capitol was demolished in 1794, and fire consumed the other in 1832. The Palace had burned mysteriously years before—in 1781, to be specific, the year the Palace was converted into a hospital for wounded soldiers from the battlefield at Yorktown—

and beside that rubble, waiting to be discovered, were the bones of forgotten heroes.

During the reign of Queen Anne had come the tragic death of her little son, for whom the Duke of Gloucester Street had been given its name. What a proud thoroughfare it had been—a President of the United States would call it "the most historic avenue in all America"— and as the dust thickened around its hallowed memories, as at times none but the old ghost reawakened the echoes of Jefferson and Washington, Patrick Henry and George Mason, it, too, appeared to wither and to die like the little boy whose name it honored.

Yet what of the genie? Whither had he roamed through these years, uncorked from his bottle, filled with the ideas that had transformed a wilderness into a colony, the colony into a partnership of "free and independent states?"

He was the genie who had whispered, "A man must have integrity, a man must have faith in what he believes is right and just."

He was the genie who had whispered, "A man must accept the responsibilities of leadership, in his home, in his community, in his church, in his state."

He was the genie who had whispered, "Government is the art of being honest, and self-government is the privilege of the man who can say, 'To thine own self be true'."

He was the genie who whispered, "All men are by nature equally free and independent, for the God who gives us life gives us liberty."

He was the genie who whispered, "Toil and thrift and

opportunity can build a brighter tomorrow for you, your children, and the children of your children."

How far from old Williamsburg did the message of the genie travel! A boy who one day would call himself Mark Twain heard these whispers, pushing a raft down the Mississippi, and around him he saw river towns bursting with the strength and industry of hard-thinking, godfearing men. Over the plains in covered wagons, down the panhandle into the vast expanse of Texas, onward and onward as the frontier was pushed to the west and the south and the north those whispers traveled—and, hearing, a Davy Crockett, a Sam Houston, a Kit Carson, a host of others, saw sod huts and open-faced cabins grow into farms and ranches. On another day those whispers were echoed by driving sledge hammers, and spikes held rails stretching from the west until they met rails stretching from the east and the country was joined into one mighty nation between great oceans.

"And that's what it all means to me," I told Father.

"And to me," Jane said.

He smiled. All good things must come to an end, and as we drove homeward bound along Duke of Gloucester Street, there was the feeling that the genie never really had forgotten the old ghost but had been so busy for a time with the whole country that he had to wait until he could get around to stirring up the will to restore Old Williamsburg to the glory it deserved. This was the genie's home, too, and he liked to have things put in order.

"Really," Father said, "this is the longest street in the whole wide world."

True, as in the old days, it seemed to begin at the Capitol and end at the College, but its idea, its spirit, its heritage stretched on and on, over the rivers and mountains young Washington had seen on his trek into the Ohio wilderness, and then beyond that over the other rivers and mountains and plains and forests Lewis and Clark had seen when Thomas Jefferson, as our third President, sent them on their famous expedition.

On and on and on—

"So reaches Main Street, U.S.A.," Father said.

THE END

REBEL'S ROOST *was composed in Monotype Bembo and printed at Clarke & Way : The Thistle Press, in New York, on paper specially made by Curtis Paper Company. The book was designed by John J. Walklet, Jr., and bound by the Russell-Rutter Company.*